Rituals
for
Resurrection

Rituals for Resurrection

Celebrating Life and Death

LINDA J. VOGEL

UPPER ROOM BOOKS
NASHVILLE

Rituals for Resurrection: Celebrating Life and Death
Copyright © 1996 by The Upper Room. All rights reserved.

All royalties from the sale of this book are donated to the Jennifer L. Purdy Christian Service and Outreach Fund of St. Luke's United Methodist Church, Dubuque, Iowa.

Cover Art: Clifford Ames
Cover design: Susan Scruggs
Interior design: Cindy Helms

Acknowledgments on pages 127-128 constitute an extension of this copyright page.

Library of Congress Cataloging-in-Publication Data
Vogel, Linda Jane.
     Rituals for resurrection: celebrating life and death/Linda J. Vogel.
     p.   cm.
     Includes bibliographical references.
ISBN 0-8358-0782-7

1. Funeral service. 2. Purdy, Jennifer Lynn, 1972-1991--Death and burial. 3. Mourning customs--United States. 4. Funeral rites and ceremonies--United States. 5. Death--Religious aspects--Christianity. 6. Bereavement--Religious aspects--Christianity.

I. Title.
BV199.F8V64   1996
265'.85--dc20

96-14995
CIP

To the glory of God
and
in memory of

Jennifer Lynn Purdy
(September 20, 1972 – January 5, 1991)

With the prayer that
families and congregations
will be helped
to share pain and celebrate joys
as they experience life and death together.

Contents

Acknowledgments

Ω

*W*hen good friends open their hearts to you and let you share their grief, you are blessed beyond measure. That has been my experience as Jennifer's parents, Jim and Mary Purdy; her brother, Christopher; and her grandmother, Rilla Stewart, have let me walk with them. Jennifer's uncle Jim Stewart also made significant contributions to this book.

I give thanks to God for the Purdy family members and for their willingness to share their story. At times I know that their reading and rereading this manuscript has been painful for them. At other times, it may have helped them continue dealing with their grief. My prayer is that they, and all of us, will grow in faith and love as we share with them the story of their deep loss.

I give thanks to God for the faith community that is St. Luke's United Methodist Church in Dubuque, Iowa. My ministry among them remains one of the great blessings of my life. Their sense of family and their continuing commitment to naming pain and growing through it are vital witnesses to what it means to be the Body of Christ.

I give thanks to God for my friends and soul mates, David Fleming, S.M., who guided my husband and me on our travels in India, and Jan Conn, whose love of music and of nature gift me each summer.

I give thanks to God for students and friends I have taught and with whom I learn. Robyn Plocher was a student at Westmar College when I was teaching there; now we are colleagues in ministry. Diane Olson, another student-turned-colleague, read this manuscript and continues to encourage me in many ways. David Otto's students from Centenary College bring much to our seminary's teaching/learning community. Lorinda Hoover was a student at Garrett-Evangelical Theological Seminary and now is a pastor in Iowa. For her and for all of the students with whom I learn, I give thanks to God.

I am grateful to God for my Garrett-Evangelical faculty colleagues, especially Jack Seymour and my eight women colleagues; for President Neal Fisher and Dean Rosemary Keller; for computer assistance from Linda Koops, Judy Russell, and Otis Thompson; and for financial assistance from a Kellogg grant (#P0026550), directed by Kenneth Vaux, that focuses on "Dying Well." The careful work of my editor, George Donigian, has been both encouraging and helpful.

I am grateful to God for my family, especially for my husband, Dwight, whose insights and moral support have strengthened this manuscript and enrich my life.

Evanston, Illinois
Pentecost, 1996

Foreword

Ω

$\mathcal{M}$ost of us live out our lives with no intention of sharing our experiences in public ways. Oh, yes, we share our stories with family and friends, and these people become our community. It is usually understood that within this community we are all fairly ordinary. With the exception of those who choose public life or writing as their profession, the rest of us expect to live and die with our stories unwritten and unpublished.

Although our stories may be moving, fascinating, or entertaining to others in our community, we don't expect that they will be of much importance or interest to those who don't know or care about us. No one would aspire to having a story to publicize such as the one our family has to share. It is not the story we had intended or imagined for our lives.

We considered ourselves an ordinary family, living and loving together. As parents, we worked hard to give our children roots, to keep them well-grounded in the sources of their identity and nurture, and to give them wings to sail off and use their strengths and talents in the global community.

However, on January 5, 1991, in only seconds, the story of our lives changed forever. One minute Jennifer, my daughter, the love and joy of our lives, was a vivacious, eighteen-year-old Rotary exchange student living in Spain. The next minute—probably radiating joy and laughter as she experienced sunshine on her face and wind blowing her curly, copper-brown hair—she was struck dead in a vehicle accident.

Several years ago our then-five-year-old nephew was diligently trying to change a directive from his parents. Lobbying with the most persuasive, unquestionable evidence he could muster, he argued, "But

I can see a movie in my head and that is not the way it is supposed to happen!" The "movies" in our heads do not play scenarios such as the one we experienced. As our nephew Thomas so logically pointed out, "That is not the way it is supposed to happen!"

Yes, certainly, when a loved one doesn't arrive home or call at the appointed time, we may imagine the scene of the sheriff's car arriving or the dreaded phone call reporting an accident. But we quickly eject that "movie" from our head and leave the remainder of the "tape" blank without thinking of how such a scenario might play out; we thrust the "tape" into the far reaches of our mind's storage shelves.

Those who approach death at the end of a long life or from the perspective of a terminal illness may project a bit more of the tape and, as we euphemistically say, "get their life in order." The rest of us go glibly along, thinking we have our lives in order as we plan our children's graduations, college educations, and weddings. Most certainly, our family was not planning a Service of Death and Resurrection for our vivacious, full-of-life eighteen-year-old. The most common statement made to us following her death was, "I just can't imagine what it would be like." That is true. It is unthinkable and unspeakable, and it is not a rite of passage acknowledged or addressed in books on parenting.

When our pastor Rex Piercy arrived on our doorstep that cold but sunshiny January day, I opened the door with mounting fear and recognition of the dreaded scene in the "movie" I sometimes, in my most horrible imagination, had glimpsed. He bore the message that we would soon receive a phone call telling us that "something had happened to one of our children." He didn't know more than that.

Christopher was in Quetzaltepeque, Guatemala, and Jennifer was in Castellón, Spain. At the conclusion of that agonizing wait, our lives were changed forever and the "movie in our head" went blank. We had no experience, no plan, no vision to lead us from that moment on—or so we thought.

Our dear friend Linda Vogel wrote this book to illustrate how Jennifer's Service of Death and Resurrection reflected the experiences and stories of our lives. We hope other people and their communities of faith can learn from our story and experience.

We had no idea when that fateful call came that "the living of our days" would be preparation for rituals of death and grief. The two people who were with us immediately, Rex Piercy, our pastor, and Ruth Ann Scott, our diaconal minister, enfolded us in their love and care and ministered unfailingly. They began the journey with us. Without their gifts and graces for ministry, there would be no story to tell.

Our family's lived experiences, which this book shares, reflect our values, hopes, and aspirations. Our rituals reflect who we are and who we hope to become. Some of the experiences that make up our story simply represent who Jennifer was. Like all of us, she was a unique child of God. She was a gift and a joy to us, her family; we have no illusion that she was perfect or without human frailties.

Jennifer seemed to have arrived in the world with her own solar pack of energy. She radiated energy and joy for life. She was an innately happy person who, like a child free-falling backward into a parent's waiting arms, trusted the universe to take care of her. An internal timer seemed to tell her not to put off until tomorrow what she could experience today.

She had never been contained by crib bars, baby gates, societal rules that excluded others, or cultural boundaries that divided. Before she learned to walk, she was able to get out of her crib or even climb onto the kitchen table and nibble chunks out of the fruit basket in the center of the table.

By the age of three, she was surveying the neighborhood and calling to her friends from the top of a twenty-foot maple tree. She had discovered that by standing on tiptoes on her tricycle seat, and stretching as far as possible, she could just barely grasp the bottom limb and shinny up the tree. Whatever the scene, she could find another vantage point from which to view it, and she always saw what others missed.

The watchful eyes and confining hands of two parents and of grandparents often couldn't keep her in tow as we traveled on vacation. Compelled to perceive through every sense, she would sidle up to human scenes that would make other children wary because of their unfamiliarity. One photo shows her at age six, sitting as close as possible to, and peering over the shoulder of, four men laughing, playing cards, and speaking Italian on a large plaza in a Boston Italian neighborhood. This may have been her discovery of language diversity.

Two years later, while we picnicked on the grassy Mall in Washington, D.C., she casually sauntered a few yards away, but within view, to sit on a park bench next to a man whose poor physical condition identified him as a street person. With intent and awe, she watched as he rolled a cigarette using a phone book yellow page and tobacco scavenged from cigarette butts. He told her he was a spider expert, she told him she was eight; and she never forgot him.

She soaked up experiences in restored Shaker villages, Amish communities, Appalachian mountain culture, Mesa Verde Indian ruins, and the midwestern farmland she called home. The Rotary exchange students we hosted, Grant Pistor from South Africa and José Fim from Brazil, became her brothers. The experience of their presence opened a new door of unlimited cultural opportunities. She developed friendships with students all over the world and thrived on the diversity.

But the mountains of Tennessee were her favorite place to be. Wearing striped bib overalls with a bungee-cord belt that honored her farming ancestral roots and her love for her grandpa, she lived out her love for others by doing service projects.

Age was no barrier either, for she had fostered friendships with young and old. While employed as a clerk in a candy store in Galena, Illinois, she became known to the owners of her favorite shops along Main Street as she stopped in for a quick chat or a bit of artistic advice.

There was no time like the present for Jennifer. Peeling paint on our barn, a nesting bird amidst the flowers, or snow mounds on a rusting farm implement were artistic photo opportunities not to be missed. It is no wonder that at the age of eighteen she had already viewed the world from treetops, mountain tops, and rooftops (while behind the lens of a camera); through the eyes of children and elders; and from the perspectives of many cultures and nationalities. She was a child of the universe and somehow had wisely known that life and time were precious.

She loved unabashedly and abundantly. This is the Jennifer her survivors knew and whose loss they grieved.

When Rex Piercy and Ruth Ann Scott sat with us to plan Jennifer's service, our thoughts and feelings were compelling, but our ability to articulate and plan were dulled by shock. Although we had no experience in planning such a service and no vision of what elements it should include, we began to express what was important.

It was important that all people—and we knew it would be a large, diverse group—feel welcomed and included in Jennifer's church home. We wanted them to feel affirmation of their presence and participation; we did not want to include any ritual or liturgy that excluded anyone because of differences in tradition.

We wanted to acknowledge that all who were in attendance were experiencing some form of grief. For many young friends, it was their first experience of death.

We all needed our anger, our questions, our doubts, and our grief to be acknowledged and addressed.

For this diverse congregation to recognize something of the Jennifer they knew, we wanted the service to reflect her many dimensions. It seemed that each person should be able to say, "Yes, that is the Jennifer whose death I grieve."

Christopher was especially clear about the music he wanted played, for it represented one of their many bonds. Her favorite hymn, a Shaker hymn, reflected Jennifer's first introduction, at age six, to Shaker society. Because she was bilingual, and her home and family the five previous months had been in Spain, we wanted some Spanish to be spoken as a symbol of God's hearing all of our voices.

We wanted the service to be a celebration of her life, and to do that it had to reflect who she was. But the most urgent, compelling message we wanted expressed was *love*—the preciousness of each day and the urgency to love one another and our God.

That, above all, was our hope.

Using this eclectic selection of secular and sacred music; our poorly articulated, compelling desires and emotions; and our request for diverse symbolic rituals, Rex Piercy and Ruth Ann Scott created a Service of Death and Resurrection that many people told us was the most spirit-filled, inspirational, consoling funeral service they had ever attended.

Many others have told us they were moved to express their love and affection to family members: a daughter was hugged by her father for the first time she could recall, and brothers verbalized their love for each other. Even through our anguish we felt surrounded by a loving community, and God's presence was felt there that day.

We invite you into our story with the understanding that it is just that—our story. It is not an example of righteous living or a story of a perfect child—for we, more than anyone, know we are not that, nor was Jennifer. We share the story openly, hoping that something will inspire you, the reader, to reflect upon the experiences of your life and to establish rituals that reflect who you are and who you hope to be. Above all, may it remind you of the preciousness of each day and of the healing power of love expressed to all persons, regardless of differences.

We continue to be surrounded by a community of family and friends who share our story and uphold us in sustaining ways. The perceptiveness of human life possessed by both Rex and Ruth Ann, their openness to God's presence and love for all, and their vision of liturgy as comfort and hope, helped create this story. There are no words to express our love and gratitude adequately to them. We only hope they realize their profound effect on our lives and our gratitude for their presence with us.

We are blessed with talented musicians at St. Luke's Church. They too shared their gifts in a ministry of love, and we are thankful.

The process of writing this book has been both painful and healing, the very nature of grief work. We have never walked alone in this journey. Among others, Linda and Dwight Vogel have been faithful in their vigil with us. We treasure and cherish their friendship and are blessed to have them share our story.

Mary Purdy
Galena, Illinois
November 1995

Introduction

Ω

Celebrating Death and Life in Community

We never know when death may come into our lives and our communities. When it comes, whether unbidden and unsuspected, or welcomed after a long struggle with illness and pain, people of faith seek to find ways both to grieve their loss and also to celebrate the life of one whom they loved. How we have learned to acknowledge and celebrate the gifts of life that each day brings will play a role in how we are able to deal with and ritualize the grief and loss that come through death.

Thinking about dying and death needs to be done in a context that recognizes the fullness of life—a context that is affirming and questioning, risking and nurturing. Paul Tillich, in "The Eternal Now," affirms a deep truth when he asks: "If [one] is not able to live, is [one] really able to die?"

Learning from "Mother"

In January 1994, I found myself waiting outside the chapel of the Mother House of the Sisters of Charity in Calcutta. Father David Fleming, Dwight (my husband), and I had been told that Mother Teresa would see us when she had finished her prayers. Soon we were blessed by the presence of this saint of our time—a woman tiny and bent of stature, with intense and compassionate eyes set deep in her wrinkled face. She spoke of the beautiful people whom those of her order had cared for as they died. "We have picked up sixty-five thousand dying people from the streets," she said. "Forty-five thousand died with us. Beautiful people—all beautiful people."

"We can now treat and even cure leprosy," she said. "Why can't we find a cure for AIDS?" Her compassion reaches out equally toward those whose lives may be saved because someone offers nourishment and care, and to those whom she and her missionaries of charity love into death.

"Please pray for us," Mother Teresa said, "that we remain faithful and not interfere with God's work." In their journey toward faithful discipleship, she knows that those who minister with her—and indeed all of us—need to be open to God, whose compassion, righteousness, and mystery can guide us beyond our limited ways of seeing and understanding. Being in touch with the world and with God's desire to enfold all peoples in justice and love seemed to me to be the sparks that continue to energize this saint of our time.

Mother Teresa and the Sisters of Charity are engaged in a *ministry of care* that reaches out to people who lie dying on the streets of Calcutta and on city streets around the world. They reach out to people suffering with leprosy and AIDS; they minister to abandoned and sick children. They do all this by seeing the Christ in each person they touch and by being willing to be present with people where they are, to touch them, to offer them food for their bodies and compassion for their souls. This ministry of care is grounded in a disciplined community prayer life, in sharing the work that is required to keep a large family functioning, and in sharing the love God has for them and for all God's children.

In the young novices who had just arrived from a grueling train trip from Bombay, and in Mother Teresa, there was a centeredness that seemed grounded in their remembering Jesus' words from the cross: "I thirst." Their task is to offer life-giving water to those who are thirsty. That is what they do.

Most of us do not live in a community that is so clearly focused. How do we, in our families and our faith communities, "remain faithful and not interfere with God's work?"

What does it mean to celebrate death and life in a world that sends so many erroneous messages about what constitutes the good life and how we might defy and deny death?

How can we be God's people: those empowered by God's spirit to offer signs of hope and love to people who thirst for real, life-giving water?

What must we do to live faithfully as a people called to be family with all the peoples of the world?

How can we name and develop life-sustaining and life-giving rituals that speak to us and for us as we experience death and live life?

Answers to hard questions can be found in the stories of our lives—Jesus knew that and often taught by telling parables and stories. In this book, we will seek to share stories that may help us discern ways in which we can be family—and community—together.

Some of the threads that make up the woof and warp of the fabric of faithful living are these:

Ω   Being present with those who suffer.

Ω   Listening with compassion and, often, in silence.

Ω   Touching and speaking in life-affirming ways.

Ω   Creating rituals that speak to us and for us about the deep hopes and wounds of our lives.

Ω   Involving ourselves in the struggles of the world.

Ω   Being intentional about attending to God through prayer, scripture study, worship, and fellowship with those who journey with us in faith.

Ω   Reaching out to those who are hurting and inviting them

to share the life-giving water of God's Word and to eat at God's table with us, experiencing God's gracious and unmerited love.

Being and Becoming a Faith Community

Paul Hanson, in a major work on the growth of community in the Hebrew Bible, asserts that community comes into being in response to God's initiating and saving activity; that it is held together by ultimate commitment and devotion to the one true God; and that it is defined by the interconnectedness of righteousness, compassion, and worship.[1] Indeed, Hanson says, "the Christian church defines its nature as church as it *becomes* church, and it becomes church as it gives up all personal claims and allows itself to be drawn, through communion with God in worship and through commitment to universal justice and peace in the world, into a reality vastly greater than itself."[2]

Jesus' ministry was not only or even primarily about saving individual souls, asserts Gerhard Lohfink.[3] Nor was it to grow churches. Jesus' concern was to gather and restore God's chosen people "in order to make this people a sign of salvation" for the entire world.[4] This restored community was to be a "contrast-society"; rather than being based on dominion-over, it was to invite and include all who were outsiders or who were victims of social or religious exclusion. Jesus' call was to a reconciled and reconciling community of care.[5]

Jesus' life and ministry was not a call to faith communities to

[1]Paul D. Hanson, *The People Called: The Growth of Community in the Bible.* (San Francisco: Harper & Row, 1986, 1-86).
[2]Hanson, 527.
[3]Gerhard Lohfink (John P. Galvin, translator), *Jesus and Community* (Philadelphia: Fortress Press, 1984).
[4]Lohfink, 28.
[5]Lohfink, 88.

save or even to enhance their own life as church. In fact, I believe that when we become preoccupied with seeking to save the life of the church, we (like those who seek to save their own lives) are in danger of losing the life with which we have been gifted (see Matt. 16:25).

We also need to avoid falling into the false dichotomy of personal salvation versus social transformation, for we cannot address personal sin and salvation apart from issues of power and social values. John Wesley was right to see personal and social holiness as inseparable parts of the whole. In fact, Wesley said, "The Gospel of Christ knows of no religion, but social; no holiness, but social holiness."[6]

When we explore what it means to develop a ministry of caring and sharing across generations in families and in communities of faith and struggle,[7] we will need to listen and look, hear and see, from the perspectives of both individuals and society. The brokenness of individuals and of social systems affects both; the healing that comes to individuals and to systems changes both. God's reign and realm is a vision that promises new life to all people and to the whole creation—until that day, no person can be truly whole. But when God's reign is fulfilled, all people will be whole. And so we are called to be God's people—in communities of struggle and faith, of righteousness and compassion, as we seek to "remain faithful and not interfere with God's work."

---

[6]John Wesley, *Works*, vol. 14, "List of Poetical Works," 321-22.

[7]In my book *Teaching and Learning in Communities of Faith: Empowering Adults through Religious Education* (Jossey-Bass, 1991), I focus on the nature and functions of communities of faith. I find Letty M. Russell's often used phrase, "communities of faith and struggle" (in *Church in the Round: Feminist Interpretations of the Church*, Louisville: Westminster/John Knox Press, 1993) more descriptive of the realities we encounter as we seek to live in faith communities.

Identity and Ritual

When we know who and Whose we are, when we have a sense of our roots and a vision for the future, we are able to share our stories and to celebrate our pains and our joys through ritual acts. Tad Guzie suggests that our raw experience becomes lived experience when we reflect on it; that lived experience may become story for us as it is shared with others; and that shared stories lead us to celebrate through festivity.[8]

It is my contention that much of what is wrong with the ritual lives of churches and synagogues today is that the festivity—the ritual acts of corporate worship—has been cut off from the personal life experiences and stories of those in the congregation, while simultaneously many no longer know or claim the stories of their faith communities. Ritual becomes empty when it does not grow out of a story that we know and claim as our own; it becomes empty when it does not connect with our real life experiences, our hopes, and our fears. So it is that for some Christians, communion or the eucharist may not be a source of nourishment and grace.

If the people do not know the stories of faith on which these rituals are based, then much of the power of the ritual act shared around the Lord's table is lost. We are gifted at the Lord's table when we experience our own breaking of bread and sharing of the cup in light of these stories of our faith:

When they invited three strangers to sit at their table, Abraham and Sarah were told God would fulfill God's promise to them (Gen. 18:1–15).

The Hebrews believed Moses and ate unleavened bread as they prepared to flee from Egypt toward freedom (Exod. 12:1–28).

---

[8]Tad Guzie, *The Book of Sacramental Basics* (New York: Paulist Press, 1981).

God fed God's people with manna in the wilderness when they were in despair and believed that they had been better off as slaves in Egypt (Exod. 16).

Elijah was fed by the widow, and her meager supply of oil and meal was not depleted (1 Kings 17).

Jesus graced the wedding table with wine made from water (John 2:1–11).

After Jesus had taught the multitude, more than five thousand people were fed from five loaves and two fish when Jesus took the bread, blessed and broke it, and gave it to his disciples to share with the multitude (Mark 6:30–44).

Jesus filled the Passover celebration with new meaning as he shared it with his disciples at their last supper together (Matt. 26:17-30).

Two disciples who had traveled to Emmaus with a stranger saw that it was their Lord when he sat at table with them and blessed and broke the bread (Luke 24:13-35).

Jesus shared breakfast on the shore with his disciples after the Resurrection and assured them of his continuing presence with them (John 21:1-17).

Knowing the stories of our faith, and how they connect with our own life experiences, means that we can celebrate the faithfulness and the grace-bestowing love of God that was given to Abraham and Sarah, to the Israelites in Egypt and in the wilderness, and to the disciples. We can celebrate what is given to us as we join others in claiming God's promise and rejoicing in God's love as we gather at the Lord's table. We can celebrate what will be given to us and to all creation in times yet to come because God is faithful and God keeps God's promises.

We know who we are—children of God *loved* and *forgiven* and *called* by God! And we know Whose we are—children of God who are called to be witnesses to God's love and care for all the world. We are therefore able to share in the festivity that grows out of our shared stories and visions. Our *identity* as God's beloved sons and daughters causes us to seek ways to celebrate and repeatedly affirm that we are who we are!

We can best learn who and Whose we are as a community of faith "not by book learning or weekend workshops, but by being present at the ceremonies"[9] as Kathleen Norris points out in *Dakota: A Spiritual Geography*. At these ceremonies, we name our pains and our joys, we express our doubts and our affirmations, we give praise and intercede for ourselves and others, we are honest together and honest before our God. Rituals that grow out of our stories and our faith community's stories, rituals that have integrity and speak with truth about the ways things really are and the ways we believe they are meant to be, can speak both *for us* and *to us* in life-enhancing ways. They can teach with great power and touch those who are open to receive God's grace.

An Invitation

When families experience a birth or an adoption, they find ways to celebrate and affirm and bless the new one who is now one of them. On our recent trip to India, I was privileged to observe a Hindu family from California who had returned "home" to engage in ritual acts and prayers with their baby. Although I did not understand the specific meaning of the rituals they were sharing with the baby's grandparents as they processed from place to place in their Hindu temple, it was clear that this three-generation family was celebrating the birth of a child they loved and was seeking blessings from One who is beyond our human existence.

---

[9]Kathleen Norris, *Dakota: A Spiritual Geography* (New York: Ticknor & Fields, 1993), 132.

Each year, we remember birthdays with a party or celebration. To have people who know and care for us share with us the joys and blessings of life is a wonderful gift. To have them share our sorrows is an even greater blessing.

When we experience significant loss or death, we need to join together with those who care for us as we seek to find ways to express our deep loss, our hurt and anger, and our hope. To have a community of care that surrounds us and prays for us and holds us up, when we may not have the strength to go on living, is a gift so great that it cannot be measured.

This book is a book of stories—experiences lived and reflected on that have become story for those who share them. It is about stories that became occasions for festivity—ritual celebrations among the people who lived the stories and those with whom they are community. Most are about Christian people and their communities of faith. One is about a family who created a significant ritual from its own family story, apart from any community of faith. All are meant to be stories that invite you—the reader—into them. It is our prayer that they may connect with or shed light on your own experiences and stories in ways that will be life-enriching and ritual-making for you and the faith community that is your own.

The rituals that are included in the appendixes are meant to be examples of ways in which ritual acts can grow out of particular stories. Use what speaks to you if you wish, or accept our invitation to create your own rituals that name your experience and reflect your faith. Dare to draw on the rich resources of your own faith tradition to celebrate death and life in your family and in your community of faith in ways that affirm who and Whose you are. May God bless you as you share and claim your stories and celebrate them with those who are your partners in community.

CHAPTER 1

Jennifer:
Her Living and Her Dying

-------------------- Ω --------------------

January 14, 1991[1]

I arrived at St. Luke's United Methodist Church early on a snowy January morning. It was cold—Dubuque, Iowa, cold! There was much activity as people worked: setting up chairs in the side hallways, working in the kitchen and dining room downstairs, making sure the sanctuary and the chancel were beautifully arranged and that the speaker system was ready to use.

People hugged as they passed in the hall. Keeping busy seemed to help a little. They had a lot to do to create a hospitable space for the family of one of their own much-loved young members. They had prepared the parlor for the family's use. Jenny's bulletin board—just as she had left it when she departed in August to go to Spain as a Rotary exchange student—was there, as well as her Bibles (in English and in Spanish) and her copy of *14,000 Things to Be Happy About* with some items highlighted in yellow. Jennifer's family had arranged another bulletin board with care. It displayed photos of Jenny and photos she had taken, along with things she treasured.

Many people had arrived at the church by 9:00 A.M. The Service of Death and Resurrection in Memory of Jennifer Lynn Purdy[2] was

----

[1]Appendix A contains a copy of the service of death and resurrection for Jennifer L. Purdy.

[2]See "Services of Death and Resurrection," 139-171, in *The United Methodist Book of Worship* (Nashville: The United Methodist Publishing House, 1992) for resources used by the congregation and family to create this service.

to begin at 10:30. But, it seemed, people could not stay away. They needed to come; they needed to be in that place; they needed to be with others whose hearts were breaking.

One of the things Jenny had missed as she celebrated Christmas in Spain was the carols. So the evergreen garland had been rehung, outlining the Tiffany stained glass "Maiden among the Lilies" window that draws our eyes above the altar and shines forth, even on winter mornings.

The chimes in the tower began playing the Christmas carols Jenny loved at 10:00 as more and more people poured into the church. Catholics, Protestants, and Jews, young and old, family and friends from far and near—all came to share their pain and anger, to surround the family and to be surrounded by love, to find hope in the midst of devastation and loss.

The melody of carols that had rung out over this Iowa river town for seventy-eight Christmases rang for Jenny on January 14! And as the notes on the large wooden console in the cold stone tower proclaimed "Joy to the World," over five hundred people trudged through the snow and entered the sanctuary where Jenny had been baptized eighteen years before.

As the last chime faded away, the organ prelude began: "Jesu, Joy of Man's Desiring," followed by "Joy to the World." Then as the casket preceded the family down the center aisle, a tape of Bette Midler singing "Wind Beneath My Wings" filled the sanctuary.[3] The Holy Spirit's presence was felt in that place.

Those who would lead us in this service stood before us and

---

[3]While some will object to mixing taped popular music with more traditional church music, *The United Methodist Book of Worship* encourages pastors to "make adaptations" and to honor "ethnic and cultural traditions" as they "work with the family in all decisions on music selection," 138. The use of both pipe organ and taped music worked well and honored who Jennifer was and spoke to all persons present.

proclaimed, "'And whoever lives and believes in me shall never die.' ...We have gathered here today to praise God, and witness to our faith as we celebrate Jennifer's life. We come together in grief, acknowledging our human loss. May God grant us comfort in our pain, hope in our sorrow, and life in the midst of death."

We heard words of scripture as the Paschal candle was lit, reminding us of the light of Christ in the midst of our darkness. Water was sprinkled toward the casket as we were reminded that "in baptism Jennifer put on Christ" and as we prayed, "so in baptism may Jennifer now be clothed in glory...."

More than five hundred voices rose as we sang "Lord of the Dance":

"I danced on a Friday when the sky turned black;
It's hard to dance with the devil on your back;
They buried my body and they thought I'd gone,
But I am the dance and I still go on.

"They cut me down and I leapt up high,
I am the life that'll never, never die.
I'll live in you if you'll live in me;
I am the Lord of the Dance," said he.[4]

(Excerpt from "Lord of the Dance" by Sydney Carter. Copyright © 1963 by Stainer & Bell, Ltd. Used by permission of Hope Publishing Company, Carol Stream, IL 60188. All rights reserved. Used by permission.)

We confessed our sins. We heard words of pardon. We stood to sing the "Gloria Patri"[5]—familiar words, often sung. These words

---

[4]Sidney Carter, "Lord of the Dance" in *The United Methodist Hymnal*, Nashville: Abingdon, 1989, 261.
[5]"Glory Be to the Father," in *The United Methodist Hymnal*, 70.

brought a glimmer of hope in the midst of our pain.

We prayed for understanding. We heard God's word:

> Comfort, O comfort my people, says your God. Speak tenderly
> to Jerusalem.... A voice cries out: "In the wilderness prepare the
> way of the Lord...." A voice says, "Cry out!" And I said, "What
> shall I cry?" All people are grass, their constancy is like the
> flower of the field. The grass withers, the flower fades, when the
> breath of the Lord blows upon it; surely the people are grass.
> The grass withers, the flower fades; but the word of our God
> will stand forever.... See, the Lord God comes with might.... He
> will feed his flock like a shepherd; he will gather the lambs in
> his arms, and carry them in his bosom, and gently lead the
> mother sheep. (Excerpted from Isa. 40:1-11, NRSV.)

We shared responsively in the psalm of the shepherd and heard
the sung response from *The United Methodist Hymnal*: "The good
shepherd comes that we may have life, and have it abundantly."[6]

Isaiah's words continued to speak to us:

> Have you not known? Have you not heard? The LORD is the
> everlasting God, the Creator of the ends of the earth, [who] does
> not faint or grow weary; [whose] understanding is unsearchable,
> [who] gives power to the faint, and strengthens the powerless.
> Even youths will faint and be weary, and the young will fall
> exhausted; but those who wait for the LORD shall renew their
> strength, they shall mount up with wings like eagles, they shall
> run and not be weary, they shall walk and not faint. (Isa.
> 40:28–31, adapted from NRSV.)

---

[6]"Psalm 23," in *UMH*, 137.

And then the congregation joined in the refrain as we heard Michael Joncas's "On Eagle's Wings":

And God will raise you up on eagle's wings,
bear you on the breath of dawn,
make you to shine like the sun,
and hold you in the palm of God's hand.

("On Eagle's Wings," by Michael Joncas. Copyright © 1979, 1991 New Dawn Music, 5536 NE Hassalo, Portland, OR 97213. All rights reserved. Used with permission.)

Jennifer's brother, Christopher, read from her Spanish New Testament, "And I will show you a still more excellent way" (1 Cor. 12:31*b*–14:1*a*). The congregation was invited to follow along in the English Bibles in the pews as we heard the "love chapter" proclaimed in Spanish.

The summer before she had left for Spain, Jennifer cared for the children of a couple who stood before us now and sang "The Gift of Love"—they raised their voices for us all—"our spirits long to be made whole...."[7]

And then the pastor prayed as he began his sermon:

We pray for strength for this difficult time.... Teach us acceptance of what we cannot understand. Teach us understanding of what we cannot change. Deliver us from the futile questioning and second guessing which come with our words, "if only." ... Keep us who sob our grief in the hand of your Son who saves us and so holds Jennifer before your throne. We thank you, Father, even through clouded eyes, that through your Son another of your children, Jennifer, lives today in the

---

[7] Hal Hopson, "The Gift of Love," in *UMH*, 408.

eternity of your house. Amen.

St. Luke's pastor, Rex Piercy, began his message, from which
I offer excerpts[8]:

Questions loom before us. Why Jennifer? Why so young? Why
this way? Why? If only... If only.... But the answers we do not
possess and no one can give them to us. We try to find some
logical conclusion. But Jennifer's death just does not make
sense. Answers to our questions we will not find. But we cannot
dismiss our questions. We are human. Our feelings and our
emotions are a part of our humanness.

On the Monday after word of Jennifer's death had reached him,
this pastor was driving across Iowa to attend a meeting. His heart was
breaking—for the family, for the church, for the things that Jennifer
would now never do.

He turned on the car radio. The Bee Gees were singing: "How
can you mend a broken heart?" That is our question. How can we
"fix it"? As words surfaced in his mind, Pastor Piercy heard from
God an answer different from the one the Bee Gees offered. "Light
of the world shine on me. Love is the answer. Shine on us all; set us
free. Love is the answer."

Even in our sorrow we affirm our hope. Our communion liturgy
proclaims that "God's love is the answer to our human fears." Pastor
Piercy continued, "We know where Jennifer is and whom she is with.
We know who we are and whom we are with." Our grief can be
redeemed in this knowledge that God's love is our hope.

---

[8]I am grateful to the Rev. Rex Piercy, then pastor of St. Luke's United Methodist
Church in Dubuque, for making his manuscript available to me. This summary
and transcription was written by listening to the audiotape of the message he
delivered.

"When you are afraid, love one another," Pastor Piercy said. "When you are all alone, love one another. When you need a friend, love one another. When you are near the end, love one another. That is God's answer."

The barrier of death is overcome in Jesus Christ. And so Jennifer's pastor concluded his message:

> Light of the world, shine on me. Love is the answer. Light of the world, shine on us all and set us free—to learn again the answer to our hopes and fears, because before that answer all our human questions grow strangely silent, and even through our tears we are able to say "Thank you, God." For Jennifer and for her life that in your love never ends. And thank you God for Jesus who is our life, too. Amen.

Following the sermon, the diaconal minister of education at St. Luke's United Methodist Church, Ruth Ann Scott, led us in an act of *naming* the one whose life we had gathered to grieve over and to celebrate.[9]

Jennifer, Purd, Purdy, or Jenny—we knew her by different names. We were to know her more fully as Ruth Ann shared with us, mining our memories and gleaning passages that had been highlighted by Jenny in her Bible and in her copy of the book, *14,000 Things to Be Happy About.*[10]

If one word symbolizes who Jenny is, it is "love." She loved her

---

[9] I am grateful to Ruth Ann Scott, diaconal minister at St. Luke's, for sharing her message with me. What is here is summarized and transcribed from the audiotape of the service. I was deeply moved as I participated in this experience of naming which Ruth Ann led.

[10] Barbara Ann Kipfer, *14,000 Things to Be Happy About* (New York: Workman Publishing, 1990).

family, her friends, her neighbors near and far, her church, her God. Almost every passage highlighted in Jennifer's Bible has to do with love and caring and serving. One of those passages Jenny marked was from Romans:

> Love must be completely sincere. Hate what is evil, hold on to what is good. Love one another warmly as Christian brothers [and sisters] and be eager to show respect for one another.... Serve the Lord with a heart full of devotion. Let your hope keep you joyful, be patient in your troubles and pray at all times. Share your belongings with your needy fellow Christians, and open your homes to strangers. (Rom. 12:9-13 TEV)

At Mountain T.O.P. [Tennessee Outreach Project], an outreach project in the mountains of Tennessee where Jennifer invested so much of her caring and loving, Jennifer lived out the gospel as she had come to know and understand it. She shared in so many ways. She worked hard, laughed often, and cared deeply.

Someone commented, "Can you say 'Jenny Purdy' to anyone who knew her and not have them smile?"

In one of her letters home from Spain she wrote: "The students are so loving, affectionate, warm, friendly. Hugs and kisses. No cliques, no nerds. I can't help but wonder what would happen if everyone at the high schools at home was equal."

In her *Things To Be Happy About* book, Jenny highlighted "getting along well with one another, teaching one another, wearing truly bag-out clothes, Kodak photography supplies...." Her photos remind us of things she loved, too: fresh tracks in newly fallen snow, old houses, old friends, a young child in a Spanish mountain village.

She also marked [in the book] "letters from close friends and far places," and "seeing happy parents." Her letters home were filled with happy memories and with expressions of love and appreciation. She spoke of her especially close bonded relationship with Christopher—a relationship her host family seemed unable to comprehend. They could not fathom the way this sister and brother laughed together in long-distance calls linking hearts in Spain and Guatemala.

She cherished a grandpa who built a rocking horse for a teenage Jennifer and who braided her hair. A grandma who let little extra hands help her with everything she did, whether it be [washing] dishes or kneading bread. Young cousins with whom she and Chris played in their tree house at Grandma and Grandpa's farm—a tree house with as many steps as there were cousins and with one of their names on every step. Aunts and uncles to love and joke with and to share lively, loving parting shots.

Jennifer left us a legacy. Jennifer sought to let inward love guide every deed, and now she's gone. So how do we make sense out of all our sorrows and all our tomorrows? We have a legacy from this lively, freckled face, tousle-headed eighteen-year-old. As Jenny's mother put it, "Find someone who needs a friend and be that friend for them."

> Our faith sometimes falters in the darkness of our lives. Hope may seem nothing more than a shattered dream. But love we have for always. Love for Purdy, her love for us. And God's deep and abiding love for us all. Yes, "faith, hope, and love abide, these three; [but] the greatest of these is love" (First Cor. 13:13 NRSV).

It was by reminding us again of the love chapter in First

Corinthians that Ruth Ann ended this time of *naming*.

Three of Jenny's adult friends—her favorite teacher, her spiritual director, and her school counselor from the Catholic high school she attended—shared their feelings and thoughts as they witnessed to what her life meant to them from their experiences with her.[11]

Barbara Ressler, her teacher, was the first to share:

> Jenny was one of the finest human beings I've ever met. Without anything resembling piety, she lived Christian ideals. Her healing, understanding, caring, and accepting nature touched many lives. And her death is a loss of losses. I don't cry for Purdy. My tears are for Jim, Mary, Chris, for all her family, for Amy, her friends, for her host family, for myself, for all who will feel a tremendous void in the absence of Jenny's tendering ways.... She possessed a heart so full of love it could not help but spill out. And it did! She reached out to the lowly, the misunderstood, the disenfranchised. She offered acceptance, friendship, healing, and hope. Wise beyond her years, Jenny lived a deep compassion. She knew life was not perfect; but she knew it was good.
>
> For me, Jenny will never be dead. Though she will no longer answer my letters,...she will live in a large way in my memory. I will recognize her in laughter and be comforted in sorrow, remembering her magnanimous understanding and acceptance.
>
> I feel impelled by Jenny's life and death. Now that she can no longer move about doing her heart-work as she did, I must,

---

[11]*The United Methodist Book of Worship* (Nashville: The United Methodist Publishing House, 1992, 149) suggests that a time may be included for persons to witness to "the grace they have received." Again, this may take many forms depending on what seems most appropriate under the circumstances.

like her, make the world warmer and more gracious.

Despair is no tribute to Jenny. She would want a living monument of love in action. Somewhere tucked in my heart, heavy with sadness, is the lighthearted Purdy, clowning me [out] of tears and into remembering fun and joy. Even in death Jenny gathers her beloved family and friends and fills us with rememberings that hug out sadness.[12]

Father John Haugen, Jenny's spiritual director, spoke next, telling us that just a week before, when he had gone on the public address system to lead the student body in their morning prayer, he had had to tell that student body that a good friend of theirs had died. He shared the feelings of the student body in the form of a prayer that they had prayed together after they had reflected on Jennifer's life among them.

It was a prayer that named the shock of death, the shadow of fear, the reminder that we, too, someday will die. It was a prayer of confession for lost opportunities to share God's love with her; it was a prayer acknowledging our need to respond faithfully and well, living each of our days to the full. It was a prayer that asked God's gracious care and support for all who grieve Jenny's death.

Bernie O'Connor, her high school counselor, shared memories of his four years as her friend. He spoke about the time during her freshman year when she and two friends came into his office with a "gift" for him in a picnic basket—it was a wiggly, black piglet! He recalled that after her graduation, "Mary took a picture of Purd and me with our arms around one another and I wished her well in Spain. When she left, she said, 'I'll see you, Bern!'" Purd was, he concluded, an embodiment of "beatitude-living."

Then Pastor Piercy reminded us that "if this were a Sunday

---

[12]Barbara Ressler's witness to Jenny was transcribed from the audiotape.

morning, it would be at this point in our service that we would
receive an offering." He invited people to come forward and offer
before us symbols that were representative of Jennifer's life, her faith,
her joy.

As the organist played Pachelbel's Canon, friends of all ages
brought forward those symbols.

A dear friend who had been her "friend in faith" (confirmation
mentor) at the church and was a long-retired speech teacher had been
asked to bring Jenny's Bible and lay it at the foot of the altar.

A family friend who had helped her select a camera with her
graduation money brought a photograph that Jenny had given him as
a gift.

A school friend came bringing Jenny's Wahlert High School
sweatshirt.

An immigrant friend from Germany, Christiana, and her mother,
Wilma, brought a jar of Nutella. They remembered that Christiana's
dad, Reinhardt, had always brought back for Jenny her favorite
chocolate-and-hazelnut spread when he traveled, and that he had
cheered her on at track meets with, "Go, Nutella!"

A church friend took Jenny's favorite overalls—worn by her
Grandpa Stewart and then given to her to wear while working at
Mountain T.O.P.—and we did not know if Ellen was going to be able
to lay them down.

Friends of all ages, whose lives Jenny had touched in so many
different ways, brought ordinary, everyday things which were
reminders of our bubbly, smiling friend who had lived as if there
were no outsiders, and laid them at the foot of the altar, below the
sun-filled window of the maiden among the lilies, there at the front
of St. Luke's United Methodist Church.

A friend of Jenny and her family who is a layperson from the
church, Larry Loeppke, then led us all in this prayer as we
acknowledged our pain and our grief in our remembering:

Dear God, You whom we have come to know as our loving parent, we come before you now kneeling and crying. You are the one who gives us our life and takes it away. All things come to pass in your oversight and care. We believe with all our hearts that you are with us, even in our darkest hour. Yet, Lord, we confess to you our tears, our heartache, our sorrow, and our confusion over Jennifer's dying.

In the midst of faith we feel resentment that this event had to happen at all, that she was taken away from us so suddenly and so arbitrarily. In the midst of hope, we feel hopeless, knowing we will never experience her smile in front of us or have her arms embrace us again. In the midst of love, we feel guilty that we failed to do all kinds of things that we imagine might have made a difference for her and for ourselves. We confess, Lord, that we need the comfort of your Son in our lives now more than ever.

We are thankful that there is someone who has laid out the path through the mystery of life and death. We know that Jennifer was before and now is a part of that mystery. We celebrate her life, Lord. We stand in wonder of her joy, her eagerness for life, her sensitivity to the world around her, and we ask you to make her joy, eagerness, and sensitivity our own as we seek to put our lives in perspective while acknowledging our loss.

Thank you, Lord, for Jennifer. We believe, without doubt, that you are loving her now just as you always have, and so are we. We pray this prayer, remembering your son, Jesus—his life, his death, and his life after his life. Amen.

The pastor then prayed the prayer of commendation: giving her back to God. The diaconal minister prayed our words of deep thanksgiving for what Jennifer meant to us and invited all those gathered in that place to join in praying our Lord's Prayer.

We all rose to sing "Pass It On"—through our tears; in spite of our tears; beyond our tears. The pain was unbelievably intense; yet we had to sing! We held one another; we raised our voices to God.

We were dismissed with God's blessing. Then the organ broke forth with the "Hallelujah Chorus" as the casket was carried down the center aisle. The light shone through the side windows—Jesus blessing the children, Jesus tenderly caring for the sheep, Jesus being baptized—and through the large window of the Ascension of Jesus.

We prayed in silence, and then the tower chimes that had called us to worship with "Joy to the World" piercing the frigid January air, prepared us to go forth as they proclaimed, "Amazing Grace." Finally, the family recessed as a taped version of "Oh, But on the Third Day," by Wynton Marsalis was played. The congregation followed as the organist played Bach's "Sheep May Safely Graze."

We had gathered to cry and sing, to hear God's word spoken to us, to pray, and to support others even as they supported us. We left that sanctuary to hug and hold Jennifer's family; we left to be hugged and held because she is a part of our families, too. We are her faith-community family; others come from her school family, her 4-H family, her Rotary exchange-student family, and more.

God's spirit was truly with us. It was named by Catholics and Protestants, by young and old, by those from near and far. There could be no doubt that God was present. Those who planned this Service of Death and Resurrection in Memory of Jennifer Lynn Purdy invited us to bring our anger and rage, our frustration and anguish, our doubts and questions, our tattered hopes and dashed dreams, and our joy-filled memories into this home of worship where we were gifted with God's spirit in powerful ways.

And So We Are Taught...

As I have reflected on this service of death and resurrection, it becomes clear to me that our *ritual acts must grow out of our lived experiences.* They must reflect honestly and with integrity what it is that has happened and is happening. They must offer opportunities for us to sing, pray, speak, and act; at the same time, they must offer us songs, prayers, reflections, and actions when we are so distraught that we cannot sing, speak, think, or move.

While some will object to mixing taped popular music with more traditional church music, *The United Methodist Book of Worship* encourages pastors to "make adaptations" and to honor "ethnic and cultural traditions" as they "work with the family in all decisions on music selection" (p.138). The use of both pipe organ and taped music worked well in Jennifer's service; it honored who she was and spoke to all the people present that day. In addition, *The United Methodist Book of Worship* suggests that a time may be included for people to witness to "the grace they have received" (p.149). Again, this may take many forms depending on what seems most appropriate under the circumstances.

A liturgy that honestly and lovingly reflects who we are and what we are feeling often speaks both to us and for us. It draws from scripture and tradition in ways that can bring comfort and hope that is beyond the deep pain and despair of the moment. When liturgy is authentic, when it reflects our deeply held beliefs and convictions, it can "bear us up on eagle wings...." On January 14, 1991, many experienced the liturgy to be authentic in this way, and so we share Jenny's story—our story—as a witness to the power that God does wrap grieving people in arms of compassion and love when we open ourselves to authentic, communal, liturgical acts.

CHAPTER 2

Connecting Across Generations

Ω

Jennifer's Uncle Jim Stewart, a Presbyterian pastor serving a congregation in Wisconsin, tells his family's experiences when they received word of Jenny's death.

January 5, 1991

Saturday began like many other Saturdays. My wife Shari was off to the school for some event related to her job. I had taken Tom and Andrew to the YMCA for basketball in the morning. After the boys and I had eaten lunch, I went outside to scrape snow off our driveway. That's where I was when Jon, my oldest, came to get me. It was about 2:30 P.M.

"Dad," he yelled, "phone call. It's Aunt Mary."

There was nothing unusual about that, but then I picked up the phone. Mary said, "Jim, I need you." The tone of her voice made me fearful.

My immediate reaction was to think, "Something has happened to Dad. This is the phone call I've been expecting."

Then she said, "Jennifer's been killed."

I couldn't believe my ears. I didn't want to believe my ears. It couldn't be, not Jenny. I asked what had happened. She briefly told me. When she was done, she said, "I need you."

And I said, "We'll be there as soon as we can." Then I hung up.

I was in a daze. I just blurted out to the boys what had happened. I remember Jon started crying. I don't think the younger two fully understood. I hugged them and bawled.

They had not seen me like that. I am sure it must have been disconcerting for them first to hear that their cousin had been killed and then to see one of their parents break down and cry. Kids are supposed to cry—not parents.

There were so many things that needed to be done, but my mind was in a fog, like being awakened from a sound sleep. I needed to reach Shari and have her come home. Someone had to take over the services at my church for Sunday.

I had better pack so that we would be ready to go as soon as Shari got home. But what to do first?

The next few hours were frustrating. I couldn't get hold of Shari. I tried the school number; it was Saturday and there was no answer. I tried her office; no answer. I called her supervisor and explained the situation to him. He would see if he could find her at the school. After a while he called back and said he couldn't find her at the school. She had said that she would stop and get some groceries, so I called the grocery store and asked them to page her. She wasn't there. Why couldn't she come home? I wanted her home. In the meantime, I tried calling our Stated Clerk [Presbyterian church leader] to see if she could take over for me on Sunday—no answer. I called the clerk of our session to tell her what was going on. She wasn't home, so I left a message for her to call me.

I began packing. I had no idea how long we would be gone, so I packed everything. The clerk called back. I explained the situation to her. She said that she would take care of getting someone for Sunday and not to worry about it.

Shari got home at 4:30. I met her in the garage. Once I told her what had happened, we needed some time to talk and cry before we got in the car to leave. Just before we left I called Mary to tell her that we were on our way. I asked if she had told Mom and Dad. She said she hadn't. She couldn't do it. She was afraid to tell them.

I said, "It'll kill Dad."

She said, "I know. I don't know what I'm going to do. I may want you to go out there. I can't just call them and not have someone there in case something happens to Dad."

After I hung up we left. In Beloit we had a flat tire. It seemed indicative of the whole day.

Finally, we arrived at Jim and Mary's around 8:00 P.M. Their friends were there. After hugging and crying for awhile, Mary told me that Mom and Dad still hadn't been told. I had hoped that somehow they would have been informed. I didn't want to have to be the one to tell them.

She asked me if I would go out there. She said that Mike (our brother) would meet me there.

I called Mike and we established our plan. He had talked with Mom and Dad's pastor, Pastor Joan. Mike would have his whole family with him. We would meet at the parsonage in Lamont [Iowa]. If he got there before I did, maybe he and Pastor Joan would go on out to Mom and Dad's.

Shari, Tom, and Andrew were going to stay with the Purdys. I wanted Jon to go with me. I just didn't want to be alone.

After talking with Mike, I called Dad's doctor and explained the situation to him and asked for his assessment on my dad's ability to handle the news. He said that he thought while it would not be easy that he would be okay. He assured us that if we needed anything not to be afraid to call him.

With our plan in mind, Jon and I took off in Jim and Mary's car. It was a long, silent trip. I kept hoping that Mike would beat me to Mom and Dad's. I drove by their place on the way to Lamont. Their lights were still on, but Mike wasn't there yet, so I continued on to Lamont.

When I got to Lamont, Mike and his family were at Pastor Joan's waiting for me. We decided that it would be best if Mike and I and Pastor Joan went first to break the news to them before Jennifer's cousins—Karen and Haley, Matt, and Kristin and Jon—came in. With that we got into our cars. Mike and Pastor Joan pulled out into the street and waited for me to take the lead. I didn't want the lead, but they obviously didn't want it either.

By the time we got to Mom and Dad's the lights were out. Mike, Pastor Joan, and I got out and went to the house. Again it seemed as though Mike was holding back waiting for me to go ahead. I am the minister, after all. He is an engineer. Maybe he thought I knew how to handle this better than he did. The door wasn't locked, so I just walked into the kitchen, turned on the lights and called, "Mom, Dad."

Mom met me. Dad was slower at getting up and was just sitting on the edge of the bed. She asked, "What's wrong?" She knew that if her sons showed up late at night, something was wrong.

I hugged her and said, "Jenny's been killed."

Mom and Dad were both shocked and grief-stricken. Dad sat on the bed holding his head in his hands, saying, "Oh, no, no, no."

Dad has always been a strong, independent individual, typical of so many midwestern farmers. He liked to pretend that he was a little rough around the edges. He enjoyed playing the role of a crusty old farmer, particularly around his educated children and their friends.

I went over to him and said, "You have to be strong. You have to be strong for Sis. She needs you."

He said, "I know. I know. I'll be all right." And he was.

Before Pastor Joan left we all knelt on the living room floor and prayed. Each one took a turn as they felt the need to say something. I was touched by the prayers of Jenny's cousins—Jon, Matt, Hayley, and Kristin. They each thanked God for what they thought was special about Jenny.

As we sat around the living room—feeling numb—Kristin, who always likes to make people feel good, climbed up into Grandpa's lap and hugged him. Later, Hayley did the same thing. It was good to have the kids with us. It was good for Mom and Dad to have some of their grandchildren there with them.

By 1:00 A.M., everyone headed for bed. We would go to the Purdys the next morning. Mike would take Mom and Dad in his van.

I woke up at 4:00 A.M. There was no going back to sleep. I got up, sat in Dad's chair, and read from Ecclesiastes. Pretty soon, Mom came out and joined me. Then after a while, Mike came down. Mom had me read out loud.

About 5:00, Dad joined us. I made some coffee and we just sat and didn't say much. I told them that I wanted to get back to the Purdys as soon as possible. I knew that Shari was the only one there with them. I wanted to be with her, and I knew that it would be good for the Purdys to have people with them. I felt a need to be there, too.

Around Mom's kitchen table, we talked. That was the place to talk. Mike agreed that I should go on ahead. He would bring Mom and Dad and the kids. So I left and drove back to the Purdys.

This is my recollection of the events surrounding the next day. I remember that day Mom and Dad coming into the Purdys' house. It seemed as though each time someone arrived for the first time there was a reliving of the events. Each time someone arrived for the first time, the tears would flow again.

I remember that on that Sunday, Mike and I spent a lot of our time trying to figure out how to get Chris home. (Jenny's brother, Christopher, was a Peace Corps volunteer-in-training in Guatemala.) He was bogged down in Miami. I remember that it was good to have problems to solve and concrete things to do.

The next week would be one long nightmare, forever etched in my memory. I remember that early Monday morning—around 5:00

A.M.—the Purdys' phone rang. It was a call from the American Embassy in Madrid. The caller was obviously Spanish and although he spoke English we had difficulty understanding each other. He wanted to know why if the Purdys lived in Galena, Illinois, they wanted the body sent to "Dubuqueee, Iowa."

It seemed as though the mornings were the most difficult for everyone and as the day went on people became stronger. That Monday morning when the phone call had come through, I felt bad because I knew Mary had been asleep. The phone call just made the nightmare come alive again for her. She cried on my shoulder and asked, "How am I ever going to survive? How can I go on?"

The arrival of Chris late Sunday night was another milestone. Chris arrived to grief, experiencing culture shock after having been in Guatemala for two months and having to reacquaint himself with the English language after having heard Spanish most of the time. The typical, cold January weather was a shock compared with the weather in Guatemala. He also arrived after a long and grueling day of traveling. But his arrival back home made everyone feel better—safer. At least Chris was home. It was comforting to know that he was with us.

Again in a desire to keep busy and do something, I volunteered to go to the airport in the Quad cities (Clinton and Davenport, Iowa; and Moline and Rock Island, Illinois) to get Chris. I think it was comforting for me to be able to do some of these things. It was a way for me to be able to deal with my grief.

One event that was very upsetting unfortunately reflects some current attitudes in our country toward the family. My wife had great difficulty getting time off work. On Monday night, Shari and I returned to Wisconsin to make arrangements at home and for our work. Shari had already used up her two emergency days. Her plan was to ask the administration for time off without pay so she could be with the Purdys. We needed to be together as a family. Her superintendent refused her request. He couldn't understand why she needed the time off. It wasn't her immediate family. It would set a bad precedent. Her supervisor said that they weren't used to dealing with people who had "old-fashioned family values." It was only when I got a doctor's excuse for Shari saying that she was suffering from emotional distress that the superintendent would agree to let her have time off.

Ω _____

Jim Stewart's recollections of his extended family's initial response to the news that one dearly loved—daughter, sister, granddaughter, niece, cousin—had been killed demonstrates many ways in which families can make connections across generations:

Ω Keeping in contact regularly by phone

Ω Thinking of others' needs and trying to respond

Ω Asking for help when we need it

Ω Calling on pastors and church friends to walk with us in our pain

Ω Including children in every way

Ω Talking around the kitchen table, crying together, hugging

Ω Turning to God's word

Ω Praying together.

_____ Ω

"For Christ's Sake, [Don't] Get Out 'a the Cemetery"

_____ Ω_____

Another family story Jim Stewart tells
offers us important insights into what it can mean
for a family to learn to celebrate death and life.

A few years ago, I served as the pastor of a small rural church while I attended seminary. The church was surrounded by cornfields. Like many rural church settings, there was a manse, the church, and a cemetery.

People stayed around the church after worship services to visit and get caught up on the news. While the adults visited and drank coffee, the kids played. One of their favorite places to play, much to the consternation of their parents, was the cemetery. The lure to play in the cemetery was enhanced partly because it was forbidden, and secondly, because there is an aura of mystery around cemeteries, graves, and death. The parents, however, thought that having kids playing in the cemetery, running around and yelling as kids do, would be disrespectful to the dead.

One Sunday morning as a mother was preparing to leave and was rounding up her children she discovered that her son was playing in the cemetery. When she saw him there she yelled at him, "For Christ's sake, get out of the cemetery!"

My family has never been good about staying out of the cemetery. I think we go there *for the sake of Christ*.

Last January when my niece, Jenny, was killed, she was buried in the Linn Grove Cemetery just west of Martelle, Iowa. Linn Grove Cemetery is like the one I described earlier. It is located out in the middle of the country, surrounded by cornfields and next to the Linn Grove Presbyterian Church.

Buried there is my great-grandfather, John Stewart—Jenny's great-great grandfather. He came to the area in 1867 and bought a farm one and a half miles north and a half mile east of the cemetery. Many of his twelve children are buried there with their families. Among those twelve children was James Leroy Stewart, Jenny's great-grandfather.

While Jenny's Grandpa and Grandma Stewart are still living, some day they will be buried there, too.

Each Memorial Day all of the family who are able gather at my brother's, Mike Stewart, who lives a half mile east of the cemetery, for a picnic. In years past, we gathered at my Uncle Dutch's, who lived on the old home place. Dutch (Delbert Stewart, son of James Leroy) died in 1981 and is buried in the Linn Grove Cemetery close to Jenny's grave.

After our picnic, we always go over to the cemetery and plant flowers on the graves of all our relatives. The Reverend Francis Marion Strange and his wife Mildred Strange, my maternal grandparents, are also buried there. Jenny knew her great-grandma Strange.

After the flowers are planted the oldest member of the family walks around the cemetery with the kids and tells family stories. We stop at each family member's grave and recite the litany of who this person was and how they are related and maybe something about them; then we move on to the next grave.

This tradition has been going on as long as I can remember. When I was young my grandpa (James Leroy Stewart) did the story-telling. When he died, my uncle and dad shared the duties. Now Dad does it. My brother and I are learning the stories and prompt Dad if he forgets some detail.

For example, David Stewart's grave is there. David was my

grandpa's older brother. He died when he was twenty-four years old. Some say he was never quite right, hinting that he might have been mentally retarded or mentally ill. No one is quite sure. Some say he started a neighbor's barn on fire and, as a result, was committed to the Mental Health Institution at Independence, Iowa. Others say he was overcome with heat and smoke from trying to save the neighbor's horses from the fire, and as a result, he became temporarily deranged.

Regardless, he was committed to the Mental Health Institution. After a few days he escaped and drowned while he was trying to cross a river getting home. Grandpa Stewart and Uncle Merle Stewart took a team and wagon to bring his body home.

This annual Memorial Day event has become an important family tradition. The cousins look forward to it. For them, the cemetery is a great place. They run and they yell. They look for the Stewart gravestones and then wait for the adults to catch up.

On January 14, 1991, when Jenny was buried there, Shari and I and our three boys, and my brother's family, all arrived at the cemetery before the hearse. The car carrying my sister and her husband, Mary and Jim, as well as Jenny's brother Chris and my parents, was following the hearse.

After the funeral service and a ninety-minute ride in the car, the kids were ready to get out and be kids. When we got out of the car and went into the cemetery, there was a sense of recognition in their faces. *They knew where they were.*

They were on familiar ground again after all that was so unfamiliar about the death of their cousin. They pointed to the different gravestones and would say, "There's where Uncle Dutch is buried, and back there is where Grandma Strange is buried." They seemed to delight in being able to tell some of the strangers where different family members were buried.

In their voices came a sense that everything was going to be okay. We would come to the cemetery in the future on Memorial Day and plant flowers at Jenny's grave and tell stories about her. Each cousin had their own stories they could tell about Jenny.

Following the committal service, I took roses out of the casket spray and gave them to different members of the family, one to Jim and Mary, one to Chris, one to Grandma and Grandpa Stewart, and one to each of the Stewart cousins. Jenny's dad marched off alone. I knew where he was headed. Together we brushed the snow off the tombstone of Grandma Strange, and there Jim laid his rose from Jenny's casket spray. He was making a connection. Grandma Strange had rocked Jenny when she was a baby. Now Jenny was with her and it was important for her dad to symbolize this family connection with his rose.

For Christ's sake we will not *get out of the cemetery.* We will go there and we will remember. We will remember that we are a family. We will remember the many blessings we have received from God. We will see the bluebird perched in front of the birdhouse Grandpa made for it, hanging on the fence near Jenny's grave, and we will hear its song. It will make us cry and laugh. We will be family, together.

We will remember these word from Ecclesiastes:

For everything there is a season, and a time for every matter under heaven: a time to be born, and a time to die; a time to plant, and a time to pluck up what is planted...a time to weep, and a time to laugh; a time to mourn, and a time to dance; a time to throw away stones, and a time to gather stones together; a time to embrace, and a time to refrain from embracing....I know that whatever God does endures forever; nothing can be added to it, nor anything taken from it; God has done this, so that all should stand in awe before [God]. That which is, already has been; that which is to be, already is; and God seeks out what has gone by. (Excerpted from Ecclesiastes 3:1–15, NRSV.)

Grandpa Stewart did die peacefully in January, 1994, with children and grandchildren keeping vigil and being included in making decisions about his treatment during his final days. Now he, too, is buried in the Linn Grove Cemetery. Uncle Jim and Uncle Mike have become this family's story-bearers.

_____ Ω _____

What a treasure this family has. They have made and strengthened connections that can sustain them in times of tremendous loss. It has required their making family a commitment; it has required being intentional about spending time together.

Memorial Day is not the only time this family gathers to share meals, remember, and tell and re-tell stories. Labor Day is "work day" at Grandpa and Grandma Stewart's farm. All the kids and grandkids come to paint, cut and stack firewood, fix fences, and clean the house—to do whatever needs to be done.

There is a wonderful old tree in the yard; Grandpa built a tree house in it when Christopher (Jennifer's brother and the first grandchild) was a little boy. The tree house has eight steps made of boards nailed into the tree's giant trunk; each step has the name of a grandchild painted on it from the youngest to the oldest. There is a favorite family picture of Jenny leaping off of her step onto an old mattress as her young cousins look on admiringly at this daring feat. It was taken during one of those Labor Day family gatherings. It reminds us all that our "family trees" are nourished when we work and play together. They shelter us when difficult times come.

The connections that were made and nourished across the years sustained this family when the pain was so great that they did not see how they could go on living. Making and nurturing connections requires intentionality on everyone's part and a willingness to schedule time for family get-togethers.

Making Connections when We Are Miles from Home

But this family has another treasure, as well. Jim Purdy's family is much more scattered across the land and there is no longer "a home place" where they can gather. Even so, they have discovered that it is possible to make and nurture connections that will sustain us in times of deep loss and pain.

It is more typical in our day to be many miles from the area where our immigrant forebears settled. Many families, whose ancestors immigrated to the United States long ago, have moved from the ethnic neighborhood or family farm settled by their pioneer ancestors. Very few of us can identify with a Memorial Day trek to a country cemetery. What, then, do families who are widespread and far from any ancestral homes do to make and maintain connections and to share rituals which can become their story? How do they make and hold memories when the world beckons us to rely on E-mail and computer-printed Christmas letters (both of which may actually have their place in our connection-making)?

The Purdy family, Jenny's dad's side of the family, is more typical of those families who have scattered geographically. Jim, Jenny's dad, had eight siblings, all of whom are married, so Jenny had sixteen paternal aunts and uncles. She was by several years the youngest of her twenty-six paternal cousins. Most of her cousins were married and had children; some of these second cousins were Jenny's age. Grandpa Purdy died before she was born and Jenny could only dimly remember her Grandma Purdy, who died when she was three. The Purdy family home was long ago destroyed to make way for another family's home. Aunts, uncles, and cousins now live all over the United States and, like most families, are caught up in the stress and pace of what we call "today's world."

Although their ancestors—including Grandma and Grandpa Purdy and three of Jenny's cousins—do in fact lie in a country cemetery, it is not realistic to think that an annual Memorial Day picnic and visit to the cemetery will be this family's ritual.

Any other ritual which depends upon their gathering together frequently won't be likely either. So what do families do? Is giving up connections, rituals, and stories inevitable and a part of reality for today? The Purdy family continues, over the miles and across generations, to nurture and maintain connections, rituals, and stories.

Jim relates that memories of the Purdy family rituals in his parental home always involved preparing and relishing food—obviously served in large quantities for a family of nine children who had relatives that visited frequently. Jim's mother, Muriel, became known as an expert cook who could make anything and everything under almost any kind of conditions. She was touted as having the world-record time for catching a live chicken, dressing and cooking it, and serving it to her family.

Obviously, she was also a good teacher, for many of her offspring have carried on the tradition of being good cooks. Even Jennifer, who never had the opportunity of receiving her Grandma's mentoring, seemed to have this "genetic" trait. By the time she was six or seven, she could use a recipe to mix up chocolate chip cookies. When they were ready to come out of the oven the cook might be hopping across the yard on a pogo stick, but she always seemed to rescue the cookies just in time.

There have been generations of Purdys and their guests who have experienced these culinary skills whenever the family gathers. One dish that has been a long-standing tradition, introduced by Great-grandmother Purdy, was a fruit-filled tapioca. No family reunion has ever occurred without someone bringing the tapioca dessert.

But the food preparation and eating was not the sole purpose of these traditions. The food is only the medium for a family gathering or celebration.

Wherever there are Purdys gathered, there is humor, jokes, nonsensical antics, and uproarious laughter. The jokes and stories are often told "on themselves," laughing without guile or embarrassment at their own human frailties, absurdities, and embarrassing moments.

It is a safe audience for singing "Rudolph the Red-Nosed Reindeer" while wearing a red-flashing light in your nose. No matter how long the separation, it takes only moments until the repartee is being dished out in helpings as large as the food. Jokes and laughter are not used to hurt or alienate; rather they bind together in pleasure and joy. A characteristic laugh and sense of humor seem to be genetic traits in this family.

Other "genetic traits" they accept with humor and grace are ears that protrude more than the average, curly hair, sway backs, a tendency to develop bags under the eyes with aging, and well-developed "gluteus maximus muscles," which account for the recognizable "Purdy gait"! All of these characteristics, at some time, are the source of humorous quips, but the big fannies seem to capture the collective Purdy sense of humor most often.

Given their heritage of cooking it seemed only natural that a Purdy Family Cookbook should be printed to capture the acclaimed recipes. Each family member in this huge extended family was urged to submit recipes. Grandma Purdy's favorite traditional recipes were included as well. The front pages are photocopies of family portraits and snapshots of homes Grandma and Grandpa Purdy and their children lived in; included also are the names, addresses, and dates of births, weddings, and deaths of the whole extended family. The famous "tapioca recipe" is on the front page. This cookbook, most assuredly, is the only one in history entitled "Big Fannies and Tapioca: Purdy Family Recipes." Each time it's taken off the shelf in a Purdy family member's home there is a smile, memories are evoked, and when "Aunt Helen's chocolate chip cookies" are baking in the oven or "Aunt Dorothy's peach cream pie" is served to guests, connections are strengthened.

Babies and children are adored and treasured in the Purdy family and each new baby in this huge extended family is welcomed as though it were the first. Their antics at family gatherings are often the source of laughter. These and other shared stories of children's antics become the folklore of the family, and the stories are told and retold.

Aunt Linda tells a story about an eighteen-month-old Jenny that she had been privileged to witness on a cherished family movie. "Jenny was supposed to be taking a nap and Mary dared to take advantage of that 'safe' time to take a bath. Jenny must have awakened; she climbed up on the kitchen counter, got the refrigerator door open, got out a full jar of jelly, and was sitting on the counter eating it with her fingers. That's where Mary found her." Aunt Linda "remembers" the story well. "Mary grabbed the camera and started filming rather than grabbing the kid and starting to yell at her or worse—as many other mothers might do."

Jenny didn't live close enough to any of her Purdy relatives to see them often. However, she seemed to be endowed with the same sense of humor. At a young age she loved to join in the repartee, using the stories she had "saved" from her experiences for her aunts, uncles, and cousins. Likewise, it was obvious that her unique, infectious giggle filled a room with light and delighted them all.

Although Purdy aunts can be as professional and decorous as the situation calls for, some of them are known to their nieces and nephews for their nonsensical escapades, which delight and amuse them. Jennifer loved these absurdities and childlike antics.

Linda shares a special shared moment that happened shortly before Jenny's death. "I remember filling water balloons with her at our last family reunion—of course there was quite a bit of water that got splashed around and never made it into the balloons."

"My last words with Jenny I just love," Aunt Linda continued. "We were standing in the kitchen at her home. We put our arms around each other and I said, 'Good-bye, you little brat!' She said, 'Good-bye, you old fart!' And I doubled over with laughter. It was so typically 'Jenny.'"

The previous August, all of Jim's siblings and their spouses had gathered in Galena—a send-off for Jenny to Spain and Christopher to Guatemala. Aunt Jean, another paternal aunt who lives in Phoenix, and Aunt Linda both tell about the time when everyone was gathered to take pictures—first the brothers and sisters alone, then with their spouses. Jenny was taking pictures with her 35-millimeter camera and Jean had her video camera. Someone called out, "Jenny, can you take a different pose?" She said, "Sure," as she turned around, leaned over, and took a group picture from between her legs. "That's Jenny!" Jean said.

Food, laughter, and family folklore—how do these stories and traditions relate to rituals of death and mourning? When the first call was made to notify the extended Purdy family of Jenny's death, Aunt Wanda, Jim's sister-in-law, was the first to answer a phone call. She and Dallas, Jim's brother, became the family messengers of the heartbreaking news.

Their first question was, "Do you want us to come right now?" and the answer was "yes." So Uncle Dallas and Aunt Wanda and Aunts Linda, Pat, and Beth came to help; they came not knowing how long the wait might be.

In the week before Jennifer's body finally arrived from Spain, dozens of people visited daily, food and flowers poured in, and the phone and doorbell rang incessantly. Family and friends needed to be together. Throughout it all, these aunts and uncles prepared and served meals to the many who gathered everyday, graciously greeted visitors, ran errands, and kept the house in order. But most important, through the tears they still kept their humor and gentle laughter. Aunt Linda and Aunt Beth demonstrated to maternal cousin Kristin how they had danced "Goofus" at the one-room school Christmas program many years before. Thomas and Andrew were entertained with some of the same kinds of antics known and loved so well by their cousin Jennifer.

As the days of waiting went on, they sat on the floor in Jennifer's room where her friends and cousins wanted to gather; there they shared "Jenny stories." Two sides of the family, who had been brought together in death, shared their stories and their grief through these rituals of remembering.

Sharing relatives long distance is another approach to family ties. Aunt Jean recalled that "one day our phone rang. A young woman said, 'This is Saskia. I am a friend of Jenny Purdy. I am an exchange student from Holland and I go to Jenny's school. When she found out I was coming to visit a friend at Arizona State University, Jenny told me I had to call her neat Aunt Jean and Uncle Lonnie.'"

When Jean got off the phone she said to her husband, "We are going to have to practice being 'neat'!" Jean and Lonnie took Saskia and her friend out for pizza. Saskia had pictures of Jim and Mary, Chris and Jenny. They shared stories and had a memorable time with "two darling girls." When Jean wrote about this experience in her Christmas letter, Jim, Mary, and Chris were surprised. Jenny had shared her far-away family with her friend in ways that strengthened family connections, and it had been "no big deal." She hadn't even mentioned it to her folks.

Jean told me that she is reminded of Arthur Brisbane's picture of a crowd of grieving caterpillars carrying a dead cocoon to its final resting place. The poor, distressed caterpillars were weeping and heartbroken. But all the while, the lovely butterfly, which had emerged from the empty cocoon they were so lovingly placing in its final resting place, fluttered happily over their heads.

It is not easy to care for such a large, extended family. There have been many griefs and sorrows as well as joys. The ritual acts of sharing food and humor are central when the family gathers to celebrate and when they gather to grieve. They are rituals which, when enacted, feel familiar and comforting because they connect those who live far apart and remind each one that distance can never negate what it means truly to "be family."

The reality that *family matters,* and that together a family can get through things that no one could dare to face alone, has become a cherished truth. Making connections across generations and across many miles is a lifelong opportunity and responsibility. It requires time and commitment. It yields strength and hope that can greatly enrich our lives. It enables family members to know that they can both be a joy to each other and, in times of deepest pain, that they will be there for one another.

CHAPTER 3

Sharing Stories And Joys And Tears

Ω

Learning To Live Sacramentally

When Jennifer was baptized at St. Luke's United Methodist Church in 1973, the congregation welcomed her into the family of Christ and into the life of their particular congregation. They promised to nurture and support her as she grew in faith. And that is what they did.

As Martin Luther knew, baptism "is a once-and-for-all sacrament which takes your whole life to finish."[1] It launches us on a journey through life with the stories, rituals, lifestyles, and values of a people who know that they are sisters and brothers with Christ and children of God.

This story-formed community offers us an identity that helps us sculpt meaning and make sense of all that we experience. Living out *of* our baptism and living out our baptism in all of our relationships is what it means to live sacramentally.

Jennifer attended Sunday school and worship with her family every week. She shared in youth activities and shared with other youth in leading the congregation in worship on Easter Sunday mornings at the sunrise services. She played "sardines" and knew the neatest hiding places in St. Luke's massive Romanesque church

---

[1]John H. Westerhoff III and William H. Willimon, *Liturgy and Learning through the Life Cycle*, rev. ed. (Akron, OH: OSL Publications, 1994), 10.

building constructed in 1896. She was a super salesperson at bake sales when the youth were raising money for Mountain T.O.P. (Tennessee Outreach Project). She was special friends with several of the seasoned saints in the church.

Jennifer loved Christmas at St. Luke's. On December 5, 1990, she wrote a letter to her good friend and diaconal minister of education: "Dearest Ruth Ann,...It hardly seems possible that it's already December and we're in the Advent season. You certainly wouldn't know it where I am. I truly miss experiencing some type of holiday season activity. Basically there is nothing relating to church, the birth of Jesus, etc." Her love of the sounds and sights and smells of Christmastime at St. Luke's was deep.

When this church first sent a work team to Mountain T.O.P., Jennifer had just completed seventh grade. She made four trips to Tennessee to worship and work, and to study and play with youth and adults from other churches around the country. She worked hard, smiled infectiously, included outsiders in ways that made everyone an insider, and identified empathetically with all the mountain folks she encountered. It was almost impossible to be around Jenny and not to feel as though you had found a lifelong friend.

When the Mountain Toppers returned to St. Luke's each summer, Jennifer joined in as the youth shared the good news of the gospel with the congregation. They talked about what they had seen and done; they shared what they had learned about what it means to follow Jesus. The folks at St. Luke's raised lots of money, commissioned the work team each time they went, and received them home with thanksgiving for what had been able to do for others and for the growth that was so apparent in the youth and adults who returned home. By supporting the youth in these ways, they were fulfilling the promises they had made when these children were baptized.

January 6–13, 1991

It was a long and horrendous eight days. Jennifer died on a Saturday. The next morning, the congregation was in shock as the news spread. On Tuesday, *The Chimes* (St. Luke's weekly church paper) included this tribute, written by one who had children Jennifer's age and who had been her junior-high youth fellowship leader:

Our Jenny

She's not gone, she's transformed among the angels
This little tousle-haired, freckle-faced girl with impish grin
When did she become a graceful, willowy woman?
How time flies!
There was our Jenny,
Stooping to dry a child's tear,
Hearing a Julia-Alex joke,
Hugging Sybil, sharing a thought,
Giving or taking a shot from a fellow Mountain Topper,
Exchanging a pleasantry with a St. Luker,
Sharing some fun in Bishops' line with a regular,
Flicking her curls, cocking her head as she was teased,
Serving her God in numerous ways.
Too brief a life!
So much love and laughter,
Inspiring a generation who loved her.
Our Jenny, and she is our Jenny,
Peers from among the lilies
Where a similar death
Silenced the members of St. Luke's,
Haunting memories permeate our worship
Binding us in Mournful harmony.
Wondering, we weep for this blithe spirit,

The very essence of God's evangel
Who lived and moved among us.

—Helen Schaub

The many allusions and one-liners in this poem reflect stories that persons in this faith community share. They are stories that include preschoolers (Julia and Alex) and seasoned saints (Sybil); they include Jenny's peers and the many other adults who knew and loved her and promised to nurture her in faith at her baptism. It alludes to Sunday lunches shared by St. Lukers at Bishop's Cafeteria. It reflects the connections with the past on which faith is built—seeing Jenny in the face of the maiden among the lilies in the stained-glass window above the altar that honors another young woman from this community who died in the late 1800s.

This poem is one woman's way of expressing for many her grief at this tragic death; it is another symbol of the way that this faith community was living sacramentally—interpreting the present in light of the past and yearning toward a faith-filled future.

Others made phone calls so that they could verbalize their grief by sharing stories or because they needed to name this awful thing that had happened in order to internalize that it was true. Some folks found ways to do something concrete—making a pie to take to the family, offering to make phone calls or to provide hospitality for out-of-town relatives and friends.

Finding ways to express our grief and honoring that there are a multitude of ways to express it—being alone or being with others, writing a poem or weeping, pounding our fist on the table or composing a song—is crucial to a healthy response to grief and loss.

The eight days following Jenny's death were ones of anger and questions, frustration and a deep sense of vulnerability. When would Jenny's body be returned from Spain? When would the service be? What can we do to help? What can we do to somehow make the pain and tears stop? Why had this happened? Why, God, why?

I was in Japan when I received the news. Denial gave way to anger and frustration and a deep need to be with those who knew and loved Jennifer. I found myself, instead, at the Peace Park in Hiroshima. It was an emotionally packed day.

I stood for a long time in front of the statue created in memory of all the children who had died in that place. Thousands of multicolored paper cranes draped the statue. As I stood there on that cloudy and chilly day, I prayed for Jennifer, as well as for all the children who had died in a flash and in the days and weeks and years that followed the dropping of one bomb.

I prayed for Mary and Jim and Christopher and their whole family; I prayed for St. Luke's; I prayed for our hurting and hurtful world; I prayed for myself. And I wept and wept.

The group I was with walked out of the Peace Park and across the bridge that spanned the river to see the monument to the many Koreans who died from the bomb—a monument banned from the Peace Park because of prejudice against Koreans in Japan. My grief turned to prayer: "Oh, Jenny. Here are more outsiders—outsiders whom you and God must love!"

Day followed day and all who knew and loved Jenny and her family grieved. People who did not know them but who had lost a child through death came or called or sent notes. And in other homes, faith communities, cities, and nations, other folks whose names I do not know were grieving the losses that were theirs.

On the Sunday before her funeral service, Jennifer's uncle, Jim Stewart, asked St. Luke's pastor if he could have a few moments to speak to the congregation on behalf of the Purdy family. Jim said, "The family wants to thank the congregation for fulfilling those vows you took when Jenny was baptized in this sanctuary eighteen years ago."

Folks in the congregation would be quick to tell you that they will always remember what they are doing whenever they participate in anyone's baptism—and especially that of babies or young children. The United Methodist liturgy asks the congregation, "Will you nurture one another in the Christian faith and life and include *these persons* [being baptized] now before you in your care?" The congregation promises that "With God's help we will proclaim the good news and live according to the example of Christ. We will surround *these persons* with a community of love and forgiveness, that *they* may grow in their service to others. We will pray for *them*, that *they* may be true disciples who walk in the way that leads to life."[2]

Never had the impact of those vows been more real and powerful. And, praise God, on the whole this congregation truly had sought to embody them and live them out in this young woman's life. This poignant moment became a teachable moment! This ritual would not soon be read by those who were present as "just a part of the baptism liturgy"! They would realize that they were making a holy vow, and they would seek to fulfill it faithfully! It is a matter of Life and death!

It was important to *name* how Jenny's St. Luke's faith family had truly done what it had vowed to do eighteen years. It helped them and helps us understand what it means to *live sacramentally*. It is in our day-to-day and year-by-year living together that we can claim the power of the Holy Spirit. Proclamation of God's promise and the vows we speak during baptismal liturgies and celebrations of the eucharist can become ways of opening ourselves to the power of God's presence so that our "talking the talk" leads to "walking the walk!"

---

[2]*The United Methodist Hymnal* (Nashville: The United Methodist Publishing House, 1989), 40.

Sacramental Lifelines

Living sacramentally means being open to receiving God's self-giving love and seeking to share that love as we interact with others in our families, in our work and school, and in every aspect of our community life. It means making and nurturing connections in ways that affirm the value and worth of all life.

Tad Guzie, in *The Book of Sacramental Basics,* describes a process that helps us understand what it means to live sacramentally. He says we all begin with *raw experience*—that is, all of our everyday actions and reactions. When we reflect on these actions, they become *lived experience.*

Our Mountain Toppers spent time each evening, before bedding down on a church floor on our days of traveling to and from Appalachia, thinking together about what we had seen and done and what we were wondering, worrying about, and hoping. This time for reflection helped all of us own and claim our experiences; for us, they became lived experience.

As we think about and talk about these lived experiences, Guzie continues, some of them become *story.* Sharing stories is the glue that binds us together as families and as families of struggle and faith. As we share these stories that have become "our stories," we enter into *festivity.* We are drawn into a celebration of what it is that we share.

There are plenty of stories that came into being for those of us who traveled to Mountain T.O.P. Some of these we were able to share with our congregation in worship and at the "stockholders'" dinner where we shared even more extensively. (The youth invited persons to "purchase stock" in support of mission trips, and this became a preferred fundraising strategy at St. Luke's. Returned missioners prepared a meal and a program for the stockholders, demonstrating the "return" on their investment.) Our stories led us to create services for the sanctuary and time for sharing in fellowship hall. Festivity grew out of our lived experiences and our stories.

Sacraments, Guzie says, are "festive action(s) in which Christians assemble to celebrate their lived experience and to call to heart their common story."[3] Our Christian celebrations symbolize God's gracious care for us; they call us to become members of the Body of Christ and draw us closer to our brothers and sisters in our faith community.

Sacramental living is rooted in the stories, beliefs, values, and lifestyles of our faith community. It is celebrated in our liturgical life together. Sacramental living calls us to nonjudgmental love because we are loved by God unconditionally; it also calls us to a radical commitment to justice which embraces the poor and oppressed. No one is outside the bounds of God's love.

Those of us who choose to root our living (and our dying) in a faith community come to know that learning to be a follower of Jesus is much more than studying and then claiming as our own the *beliefs* of the church. It involves learning the stories of our faith (Bible stories, stories of the church throughout the ages, and the stories of our own denominations and congregations) and then discovering how our own life stories connect with these stories of our faith. It impels us into celebrating these stories as we engage in the worship and ritual life of our faith community and our family.

When we baptize and marry, when we pray for forgiveness and for healing, when we grieve our losses and celebrate the lives of those who die, we are calling to consciousness the sacramental quality of our lives; whenever we gather around the Table to break bread, and to remember and participate in the redemptive power of Christ, we are witnessing to the sacramental nature of all of life. All of these acts draw us into our faith's story and connect us with the all-inclusive, justice-seeking love of God which holds and nurtures us

---

[3]Tad Guzie, *The Book of Sacramental Basics* (New York: Paulist Press, 1981), 53.

when we are in despair, challenges and empowers us when we become complacent, and judges and chastises us when we forget who and Whose we are.

We remember the stories of our faith:
stories of Abraham, Sarah, and Hagar;
of Hosea and Gomer;
of David and his wives, sons, and daughters;
of Naomi, Ruth, and Boaz;
of Mary, Martha, and Lazarus;
of Peter and Paul;
and of Mary Magdalene and Lydia.

We remember Jesus and the ways he reached out:
to women;
to Samaritans;
to children;
to lepers;
to a rich young ruler;
to tax collectors;
to the multitudes;
and to the religious leaders of his day.

All of these stories and so many more can become our stories as we hear and feel what it means to be a part of the human family. These are not pious stories of right-living, unreal people. These are stories of fathers and mothers, sons and daughters, kings and outcasts, of everyday human beings like you and me. They were heroic and self-centered, greedy and generous, self-righteous and self-negating, open and closed, pompous and humble. Biblical stories reflect families that are broken (as *all* our families are), faith communities that are being torn apart by conflict, and real differences of opinion about what it means to worship and serve God. When we encounter the stories of our foremothers and forefathers in faith, we see ourselves and our struggles, our questions and our doubts, our hopes and our attempts to walk in faith.

Sometimes we are like the Pharisees—concerned with the letter of the law outwardly while missing the capacity to love and be loved unconditionally. Sometimes we want to be healed but are like the man who had been lying by the pool for thirty-eight years waiting for someone to come along at just the right time (John 5). Sometimes, like James and John, we get caught up in questions of our own importance.

Hearing and telling and re-telling the stories of our faith can become a mirror for us. We can see ourselves and others in light of God's great love, and we can hear God's call to us—individually and collectively—to journey together in faith toward God's realm where justice and peace for all creation can become a reality.

When we choose to live our lives within a faith community, we find that our sisters and brothers offer their *presence, hope,* and *comfort;* this can see us through our deepest despair and unfathomable hopelessness during those times when we must face tragedies of life that seem to us to be beyond our ability to withstand. When words seem to have no power and all seems beyond our ability to go on living, the Holy Spirit moves through the community of those who are bound together by the stories of faith, and sees us through.

It was the St. Luke's faith community which was present with Jim and Mary and Christopher. We held them in our arms and cried with them. We did not have an answer to Mary's question, "How can I go on?" But we offered our presence and held each other up because we knew we were all surrounded by the embracing love of God.

There are many, many ways in which to learn and share the stories of our faith. We hear them read at bedtime when we are children and from the lectern in worship each week. We sing them in worship and around campfires. We recite them in our rituals of baptism and the Eucharist; we proclaim them in our creeds. We study them in Sunday school or CCD and in confirmation or membership classes. We act them out during Vacation Bible School and at camp. We participate in Bible study classes in our homes and churches.

As we mature in our faith journey, we learn to find connections between the stories in the Bible and our own life experiences and stories. Proclamation of God's word in worship needs to challenge us to make these connections as well.

When do we, like Moses, argue with God and claim that we do not have the ability to do what God wants us to do?

When do we misunderstand what it means to be in ministry—wanting others to wash our feet rather than willingly washing the feet of those who are dusty and tired from journeying through life?

When do we exclude those who do not keep the "law" as we understand and interpret it?

When are we like Nicodemus—trying to understand, while still protecting our position in the world?

When will we finally recognize that doubt and unbelief do not exclude us from the community of faith and that Jesus honors our prayer: "I believe; help my unbelief" (Mark 9:24)?

Embodying Sacramental Living in Our Faith Communities

As soon as the pastor and diaconal minister began talking with Jim and Mary and Christopher about plans for Jenny's service, it became clear that foremost in Mary's mind was the need to create a *warm, nurturing, and hospitable space* where all who came would know that they were welcome. Whoever knew and loved Jenny must experience this church as a people and a place where everyone is accepted as they are; we must treat each one who comes as a cherished child of a loving God.

Flowers in the parlor, an inviting dining room with time to share at table, and a sanctuary that offers hope and a community of care must be the way persons who come experience this place. For Mary, it was as if these hundreds of persons were to be guests in her home. The care and attention she gives to making guests feel welcome there is what she expected of her faith family on this day.

The Purdy family brought Jenny's bulletin board to the church parlor and arranged a display of some of her treasures. They were acting out of a deep knowing that if they and others were going to survive this day of Jenny's funeral, we would have to be reminded of and share "Jenny stories." Others who were there contributed to the memory bank as we stood among her things and shared our own "Jenny experiences and stories." Even those who knew and loved her best saw her in ways they had never seen her before. Sharing stories—family stories, Mountain T.O.P. stories, neighborhood stories, high school stories, church stories, babysitting stories—that were funny and sad, moving and ordinary, were lifelines to the Jenny we had each known and loved.

Jenny had bid her church family good-bye in August as she embarked on a great adventure; Jenny had written and received lots of letters from many friends; she had talked and laughed with her extended family on Christmas. Now Jenny's lifeless body had finally arrived from Spain and was in a closed casket upstairs at the back of the sanctuary. We reminisced and cried and smiled as we remembered together the stories of times when Jenny had touched our lives.

The chimes in the church tower were playing carols she loved and had missed that year at Christmas. These rang out the promise of God's gift of love and hope for all the world. We rang them for Jenny; we rang them for ourselves on this cold January day because we, too, needed to hear the gospel proclaimed in ways that would speak to our broken hearts; we rang them as a witness of our faith to a community that also cries out in pain and longs for peace and wholeness.

The memory of this witness continues to be remembered and the story continues to be told. Mary gives Jennifer's friends little nativity sets as gifts when they leave home for college—"Remember," she says, "you can always carry your tradition with you wherever you go." This is sacramental living.

The blending of classical religious music, contemporary Christian music, and jazz that was used in Jenny's service reminded us that there can be no separation between the sacred and the secular. We listened and were comforted because we knew that this music which had spoken to her now spoke for her to us. It spoke in traditional words of scripture and faith and in the words of the world of her young peers.

In Jennifer's service, the lighting of the Paschal candle and the sprinkling of water toward the casket reminded us of her baptism and ours. The pastor reminded us that "in baptism Jennifer put on Christ" and prayed that "in baptism may Jennifer now be clothed in glory." These words and this ritual act provided brackets around what it means to live out of our baptismal vows.

When we are at a loss for words, familiar words of scripture can comfort us and bind us together. When our world seems to have spun out of control, we can hang on to God's word; it offers us hope and the promise that God will not abandon us in our despair.

The Spanish Bible that Christopher used to read the "love chapter" from 1 Corinthians has a history, too. The church had received a new pastor in June before Jenny left for Spain in August. That is not long to create a connection with an eighteen-year-old. But Pastor Rex Piercy had done so. He came to know her, and when she was ready to leave for Spain, he gave her a Spanish New Testament that had been given to him. It now contained two inscriptions! This Bible reminded all of us that the world is bigger than this time and place. It linked us to Jenny's other world and family in Spain—a world where hundreds of people had gathered the week before to celebrate a mass in her memory in the tradition of their faith. It reminded us of the link between Jenny and her Spanish family; it reminded us of the link with Chris's new Peace Corps home in Guatemala.

These two St. Luke young adults—sister and brother—had acted on their baptism to reach out to persons in other lands who spoke another language but whose lives were being touched by the power of a gospel of love and care. This simple act of reading from Jenny's Spanish Bible reminded us of a whole network of friendships and worlds of nurture and care. It reminded us that understanding God's message comes first through acts of love; our words can remind us and help us name those acts. Words alone—empty words—lack healing power.

Living out our baptism invites us to name for ourselves, for our families, and for our faith communities the pain, anger, frustration, and deep wounds that are ours. Pastor Rex and Ruth Ann did that for all of us at Jennifer's service.

Those who live sacramentally cannot avoid or deny the reality of deep loss, of betrayed trust, of experiences that defy our ability to understand. Living sacramentally invites persons to grapple with Truth, to speak our doubts, and to shake our fists in anger. The psalmists model for us this kind of honest confrontation.

For Christians, coming to experience the power of the Eucharist requires us to come face to face with betrayal and undeserved death. We can move beyond the fear of death only by experiencing and coming to know that Jesus Christ gave his life to save all peoples and that God's great love comes to us through this self-giving act of love. Claiming this gift often requires us to walk through valleys of death; it is then that we know most clearly that God's love is greater than the power of even death and can never be destroyed.

The section of Jenny's service that helped us enter into *naming* invited us to recall experiences and stories that called us toward a deeper, more faithful way of living. There were Jenny stories, family stories, and school and church stories that connected us to her worlds and to our world at a time when many of us felt as if we were suspended in a twilight zone.

The Mountain Toppers had experienced so much together that their experience provided a rich core of stories and songs; these in turn reminded the youth and many of the adults at St. Luke's of more people and stories and songs. "It only takes a spark to get a fire going" was a word that we needed to hear. Seeing how Mountain T.O.P. had helped Jennifer reach out to friends outside this faith community and invite them in, could be seen in Christiana's gift of a jar of Nutella (chocolate-and-hazelnut butter) laid at the foot of the altar, along with Jenny's grandpa's overalls, which she had worn often at Mountain T.O.P.

These gifts tied together strands in Jenny's life that reached from Spain where she was killed; to Wahlert High School in Dubuque, Iowa; to Mountain T.O.P. where Jenny, Ellen, Christiana, and so many others had worked and prayed and grown in faith together; to St. Luke's which was Jenny's church family. It was this faith family that now welcomed and invited into remembering, crying, and thanking God, all these folks who had been touched and were being touched by one who lived life as if there were no outcasts!

Jenny's school family came to this place from a different faith tradition. These Roman Catholic teachers and classmates had helped her learn what it might mean to be "one holy catholic and apostolic church." (And she had certainly broadened their perspectives, as well, as she interpreted Protestantism and embodied "being United Methodist" in their midst.) Although it is sometimes painful to be reminded that Christ's table is not always open to all, sharing in the worship and ritual life of persons from differing traditions can teach us ways to create rituals that can become bridges rather than walls.

Singing, praying, crying, listening, seeing—together we were all gifted and comforted by this time when we came to know Jenny more fully than we had ever known her before. We knew, too, that the God who loved Jenny, and in whose presence she was now for eternity, loves us also and will see us through this valley of death in which we have dared to walk together.

Our worship was an expression of sacramental living. The sacramental living continued as we gathered around tables in the church's fellowship hall to remember and share stories with our friends and with those who were strangers to us but with whom we could share deeply because they, too, were Jenny's friends.

Getting beyond Roadblocks to Sacramental Living

Why is it that we so often fear sharing our stories and joys and tears? Why do some folks leave the church when the going gets tough? Why can't we share our pain and allow ourselves to be held and cared for? What bad things have happened or do we fear will happen that stop us from being vulnerable and crying out?

Sometimes we buy into addictive and destructive behaviors that are applauded by a culture controlled by guilt and driven by its gods of overachievement and perfectionism.[4] Too often we "wear masks" when we go to church, wanting our family to appear intact and healthy. Sometimes we fall into the "if only" trap; this blocks us from naming and dealing with the realities that face us.

We may fear being judged; we may feel guilty and suppose that if we had done certain things differently, we would not be experiencing so much pain. There is a tendency to believe that good people do not experience what we are experiencing. Because we

---

[4]See Robert Hemfelt, Frank Minirth, and Paul Meier, *We Are Driven: The Compulsive Behaviors America Applauds*, Nashville: Thomas Nelson, 1991 and Stephen Arterburn and Jack Felton, *Toxic Faith: Understanding and Overcoming Religious Addiction*, Nashville: Thomas Nelson, 1991.

cannot accept ourselves and our situation, we assume that others could or would not accept us either. That assumption blocks us from lifelines of hope.

We may have been taught that certain questions are beyond asking if one is really a "good Christian." Even if we were not taught this overtly, we may still have learned that if we really have faith in God we will not have doubts or feel certain ways. This leads us to suppress or, at least, not to voice our doubts and fears. It blocks us from asking hard questions and then struggling with them—in community, with other persons of faith.

When we—or those with whom we dare to share our questions—assume that questions are to be answered rather than to be lived into, we tend to short-circuit the process. Listening with empathy and walking into another's hard questions with them is what persons need. Our answers may not be another's answers and, even if they are, they need to discover these answers for themselves and live into them in their own time.

A hospital chaplain, on call one night, was called to be with a middle-aged man whose father was dying. The son was very distraught. The chaplain sat with this man as he told the anguishing story of his stormy and painful relationship with his father who now lay dying. The son expressed rage and remorse that things could not have been different; he named the feeling welling up in him that he was not sorry to see his father die. The chaplain listened; he held the man when he sobbed; he was present.

The next day, the chaplain was surprised to discover the man waiting for him in his office. The man said, "How can I ever thank you? I've finally found a priest who had some answers!" And, the chaplain breathed a silent prayer as he accepted the man's thanks; he knew in his heart that, thankfully, he hadn't said a thing. The "answer" was in his caring and in his receiving, in his being present and accepting. In that safe and hospitable space, God's spirit had provided the deep answer that brought peace to an anguished soul.

Many times, the answers we give to a person in pain are a block rather than a lifeline. What people need is our *presence*—open, dependable, nonjudgmental, empathetic. We are all called to share our journeys in and toward faith—honoring each one's questions, doubts, hopes, and tentative steps toward wholeness.

When we cry out, "Why, God, why?" there is no answer. What we need are arms to hold us, someone who loves and cares to cry with us, and a safe place to be. We need to know that God listens and cares and cries, too! We need to know that God comprehends our anger and does not desert us or punish us because of it.

Now is not the time for a theological treatise on how God is able to receive our anger and still embraces and cares for us—even when we claim to deny God's existence or turn our back on our relationship with the God who creates us, who loves and cares for us, and who calls us beloved friend. Rather, those in our faith family can re-present God's love and care and acceptance by being present in nonjudgmental ways and by encouraging us when we name our anger or express rage toward God.

Sometimes funeral services can be roadblocks to sacramental living. This happens when the service is an empty ritual that is disconnected from the gospel story and the meaning that comes when both individual and faith-community stories intersect with the gospel. I have been present at services that focused so much on the resurrection of the one who died, that I could not get past my own anger and pain and loss to participate fully.

I believe that Jennifer's service nourished us when our hearts were breaking for several reasons:

We knew that we were called to focus on God and God's
gracious love as we worshipped.

We were honest—crying out our anger and helplessness in ways
that let us also hear God's word and celebrate the deep joy

Jennifer had brought into our lives.

It was participatory—calling on all of us to sing and pray, using the prayers, songs, reflections, and ritual acts of many of her friends and loved ones on behalf of us all.

These are principles that can help faith communities find ways to celebrate death and life with integrity and hope. Funeral services must truly acknowledge the pain and deep loss that death brings; at the same time, they must breathe words of hope and the possibility of a hope-filled future. Meaning must be built around the stories and vision of the faith community as they intersect with and connect to the deep feelings and experiences of those who have come. Then it is possible to celebrate the life and grieve the loss of one for whom they cared.

There is a time to cry and a time to be comforted. There is a time to grieve and a time to celebrate. Somehow our services of death and resurrection need to provide the community opportunities to acknowledge and express both ends of the emotional spectrum.

Liturgy that "speaks the truth in love" fosters sacramental living. These liturgies must have integrity; we cannot ignore or lie about situations that caused deep hurt and pain to family members and friends. Neither should we use liturgy to "get back at" one who died and whose own life was filled with woundedness and pain.

Rituals can be doors into new beginnings. That is true for baptisms, eucharistic services, and other rituals that we create to speak to us in particular life situations. There are many ways in which we can invite families and those in our communities of faith to remember grief and loss and then to accept the love and support of others. Together we can move beyond that grief and loss toward new beginnings.

Ω _____

Some Guidelines for Living Sacramentally

Living sacramentally is a life-long process that invites us to:

Ω Be in touch with our own feelings, thoughts, joys and fears.

Ω Reflect on life's experiences and create the stories of our own autobiographies.

Ω Listen to the stories of the faith community of which we are a part and make them our own.

Ω Hear them as stories in which we all participate.

Ω Identify with these foremothers and forefathers in their weaknesses and their strengths.

Ω Identify connections between the good news of the gospel and the questions and affirmations of our living and dying in families and communities of struggle and faith.

Ω Find ways to share and reflect on those stories of faith which have become and are becoming our own stories.

Ω Participate in community celebrations (including worship) that honor the gospel story and our own stories—including our fears, our hopes, our questions, and our answers that no longer satisfy us and are replaced with even harder questions.

Ω Continue to participate in singing, praying and listening to the

proclamation of the gospel, even when our own questions
overwhelm us and draw us away from the community that
can sustain us while we feel cut off and disconnected.

Ω Persevere in asking the hard questions and searching for the
truth that is never threatened by the hardest and most
persistent questioning.

Ω Live into our questions and insist on honesty and patience
from those who walk with us on our journey into and through
our questions.

Ω Celebrate the little victories along the way so that we can be
energized to continue journeying through the pain and
questions toward wholeness.

Ω Thank God that being and becoming faithful is a gift that
God gives.

Ω Journey with the assurance that God loves and cares and
walks with us in and toward God's "household of freedom."

_____ Ω

CHAPTER 4

Authenticity Is a Key

Ω

*P*lanning Jenny's service to grieve our loss and to celebrate her life with us and her resurrected life with God was both terribly painful and deeply comforting. Because those who planned it could draw on the rich resources of the Christian faith and on the wonderful gift Jenny had been to so many, the planning and the service itself could be a source of comfort and hope. They were a part of the family's and the faith community's grief work.

But what happens when we use words like these to mask truths that seem unspeakable? What happens when we go through the motions and read scriptures that were not a part of the belief system or the life practice of a person who has died? Is there any comfort for anyone in that? And if there is, is it a sham that helps people escape from facing their own futures in authentic ways?

I believe it is possible to be both *compassionate* and *authentic* as we seek to create and celebrate rituals that reflect the way things have been, the way they are, and the way we are trusting they can be. I believe the God of Abraham and Sarah and Hagar, the God of Peter and Paul and Mary Magdalene and Lydia, is the God who longs to enfold all peoples (including you and me!) in arms of compassion. I believe that compassion is linked to God's call to us to be God's instruments of justice and care in the world. This compassionate and challenging God requires us to claim our identity and to speak and act authentically as we share our stories and celebrate who and Whose we are.

Creating Liturgies that Speak to Us and for Us

It is this drive for authentic ritual that led a good friend of mine, Robyn Plocher, to create a liturgy that she knows she and others like her need. She has been struggling with life after childhood sexual abuse, perpetrated by a clergyperson and family member. She is growing toward wholeness (as are we all!), and part of her healing process has been to create a liturgy to be celebrated with close family and friends at the death of the perpetrator of abuse. This is a resource that is very much needed in our churches and families. She offers it to the church (see Appendix B) as an example of a liturgy that is both honest and compassionate.

Grounded in the service for the "Congregational Reaffirmation of the Baptismal Covenant"[1] in *The United Methodist Book of Worship,* this liturgy demonstrates one among many settings in which Christians are invited to affirm God's grace and the reality of new life in Jesus Christ. We participate in remembering and claiming once again the gift God gives when we die to self and are raised as blessed children of God through the sacrament of baptism. While the sacrament of baptism is once-for-all, living it out takes a lifetime. This reaffirmation liturgy can help Christians and congregations remember the vows they take at every baptism and can empower each person to focus again on the meaning of faithful discipleship as the Body of Christ—the church.

When Jim Stewart thanked the St. Luke's congregation for having fulfilled the vows they took at Jennifer's baptism eighteen years before, those vows—sometimes recited in a rather routine way—suddenly came to life. Likewise, the power of this liturgy Robyn created will help all those who share in it to see connections between what we do in baptism and what it means to live

---

[1]*The United Methodist Book of Worship*, Nashville: The United Methodist Publishing House, 1992, 111-114.

intentionally as a claimed child of God within a faith community.

This liturgy for "A Memorial Service for Survivors of Abuse upon the Death of the Perpetrator" speaks to those who experience both relief and grief at the death of someone they both hate and love. It proclaims God's love for them and God's presence with them; it announces that the Church is willing to stand with us as we name and claim who and Whose we are—with all our pain and our joys, our wounds and our gifts. There is nothing that can separate us from God's love in Christ Jesus! This we proclaim with certainty! It is a liturgy meant for a small group who knows, is trusted by, and is able to support one who experienced abuse at the hands of the deceased.

In Robyn's liturgy, the renewing of one's baptismal vows is a powerful reminder that we are made new in baptism and can remember that as we renew and reclaim God's gracious and lifelong promise that we are always being made new when we walk in faith. Christ—who is "the dance" that will "never, never die" and who will "live in [us] if we will live in [Him]"[2]—gives us the strength we need to be healed: healed of our grief, healed of abuse, healed of all that separates us from God's empowering love. When we dare to "remember our baptism and be thankful" we are living sacramentally.

Robyn's liturgy has power because it affirms that "before you were *[father's name]* or *[mother's name],* you are Mine—a child of My own creating, precious in My sight. My grace is sufficient unto the need." It focuses on claiming one's place as a beloved child of God and a member of God's own family. It insists that we remember the good times and the bad times that were shared with the one who has died. It draws on scripture and hymns of faith that do not gloss over the violence and betrayed trust. Rather, they acknowledge what has been in the past and invite us to walk through that pain toward wholeness.

---

[2]Carter, "Lord of the Dance."

This liturgy is not meant to replace a funeral service for the larger community. That service could draw on the resources of the faith community to speak in truth (though not the whole truth) to those who come. That service should *not* lift up the person as "a loving and devoted family member" any more than it should make public particular sins of abuse. It might focus on a God who loves and forgives and promises to make new all those who open themselves to God's transforming love. *Compassion* must be bonded with *integrity* in all our liturgies if they are to speak to us and for us with power.

There are many other life crises and life transitions to which a baptismal renewal liturgy can speak with power. For example, it was out of the lived experience of older individuals who had lost spouses that a class studying older adult ministry taught by David Otto at Centenary College in Shreveport, Louisiana, developed a ritual for use some weeks or months after the death of one's spouse (see Appendix C). In it, family and friends gather to pledge support and to symbolize through the use of water and holy touch the promise of new beginnings.

While this liturgy was designed with older adults in mind, it shows us how we might go about creating liturgies for a variety of "new beginnings." We see again ways that liturgy can help us express both grief and hope as we plan and then share in ritual acts as a community of faith, whether through a small group which represents the whole congregation or within the context of congregational worship.

Another friend who was doing CPE (Clinical Pastoral Education) in a hospital setting found that she needed an ecumenical service of Christian baptism for infants and children who were in danger of death. Lorinda Hoover drew on resources in the *Book of Common Worship* (1993) of the Presbyterian Church (U.S.A.) and *The United Methodist Book of Worship* (1992) to design a modular service (see

Appendix D).

Because most Christian traditions consider baptism in extenuating circumstances to be valid if it uses the triune formula and includes the use of water, Lorinda retained the traditional formula rather than using a more inclusive trinitarian formula, which is her personal preference. This service is meant to be adapted by the user so that it is appropriate to the context and pastorally sensitive.

These liturgies, which are included as appendices, offer models for creating liturgies that grow out of particular life experiences and needs. They reflect who and Whose we are and offer us opportunities to name our pains and our hopes in the presence of faithful brothers and sisters; they invite us to claim God's gracious promise of God's all-embracing, justice-seeking love. We and all creation will be gathered under the wings of a loving, nurturing, protecting God who, like a mother hen, will surround and never forsake us.

Creating Kaleidoscopes

Some of us may be inclined to say, "But the Purdy family is different. They have something special." Connecting across the generations is also possible for families that have not always remained closely connected. It is possible for those who have lost family stories and who have not maintained close ties to reconnect in powerful ways. It is also possible for families who are not nourished by and connected to a faith community through church or synagogue to reconnect with one another.

As I was working on this book, I received a seven-page letter from another dear friend. Jan Conn thought I would be interested in what she had written for her family's "Heritage Day." Her family is scattered across the United States; in addition, it has skeletons in its closet—suicide and mental illness and extreme reclusiveness are a part of their history.

When one of Jan's grandnieces announced her marriage, Jan and her two sisters decided it was time to plan a family celebration. The niece's great-grandmother (Jan's mother), had she been living, would have celebrated her one-hundredth birthday in 1991. A person doesn't have to be alive in order to have a birthday celebration, they decided.

Because the grandchildren had always experienced Jan's mom "lying on the couch" and quickly "excusing herself and retreating into the back regions of the house" (to use Jan's words), they had never really known their grandmother. They had never "had tears wiped away by a sympathetic grandmother." Further, there was a certain "mystery" about her—sometimes family members would accompany any mention of her name with "a perplexed shake of the head." This side of the family was rarely the subject of stories told and memories relived. The time was ripe, it seemed, to try to plant memories and to claim stories from this side of the family. So Jan and her two sisters made plans and extended invitations to family members.

They wrote, "Our tales of old are no more exceptional than those you all share with your own siblings and cousins, but we thought it would be fun to get together and pass on some of those old tales and facts from a side of the family" that had rarely been shared.

Occasioned by the marriage of Jan's grandniece, the family of this reclusive grandmother gathered to hear stories and to receive "treasures and their stories" that her three daughters chose to pass on to the next generations. As these three sisters sought to link past to future, Jan decided that "we should have some physical object created especially for this day" to remind each one of their heritage and of their own personal place as a bridge between the past and the future. And so she made kaleidoscopes for each relative. Here are her thoughts as she wrote them in her family letter:

> It came to me that the most appropriate thing I could think of was a kaleidoscope. A child's toy, you say. A few flecks of bright color free to tumble at random, and the resulting pattern

reflected in a triangular system of mirrors: *kaleidoscope*. The word is from the Greek "kalos" (beautiful), "eidos" (form), and "scope" (an instrument for seeing).

To me this is more than a child's toy. It is a lesson in genetics. Each of these bits of color represents a family characteristic we have inherited from our parents. We three sisters have the same genes from ancestors known and unknown. Why aren't we all alike? Because like a kaleidoscope, each of us has been tumbled into a different pattern. Although we each have characteristics identical to those of our sisters or parents, our pattern is unique to us. No other person has these characteristics arranged in just this way. Each of us is different from anyone else who has ever lived, and yet we have qualities in common with folks we will never know.

As you look through this kaleidoscope you will see that some colors are jumbled one on another so that their original color is altered. So it is with our characteristics. We combine qualities and create a new trait. Some fragments in our personal kaleidoscope drop down below the level of the reflecting mirrors and are not in evidence at all. Is this what is being referred to when we are told that we use only a fraction of our potential? Are those hidden qualities actually available to us? Or do we only pass them on to future generations, until in combination with the genes of the families we and our descendants marry into, they suddenly pop into view and form the centerpiece of yet another unique pattern?

Thinking of the colors in these kaleidoscopes as family characteristics I began to feel as if I were playing God as I gleefully snipped apart plastic pop bottles, cheese and oleo containers, grocery ties, a car bug-shield, and one red, broken glass tumbler.

What sort of people was I assembling? Did red portray

courage or hot-headed anger? Was yellow a sign of cowardice or simply a sunny disposition? Was blue an indication of a cold personality, steel-like strength, or a depressed frame of mind? The single piece of glass—so fragile and at the same time so sharp of edge—will it be broken amid its tumbling neighbors, or will it cut them all to shreds? What puzzles we all are.

There are fifteen fragments in each kaleidoscope, three each of red, blue, green and yellow. Of orange (a rather hybrid color perhaps on its way out) only two. That comes to fourteen. Did I say fifteen? What about that fifteenth piece? We'll learn more of it later.

As I look at our family I see people of intelligence but not genius—although a few have come close.

We are not flag wavers nor are we easily swept up in mass movements and wars.

We are slow to anger and tend to avoid confrontation to the point of being walked on occasionally. But when we are roused and have strong feelings, we are tenacious and stubborn. The tenacity serves us well in carrying difficult projects through to completion.

More often our drive is in the field of ideas and our goal the satisfaction of a job well done, rather than wealth or power. However, the desire for acclaim is strong (too strong, maybe) in some of us.

We are not charismatic leaders or trendsetters. Neither are we trend-followers. We prefer to go quietly our own way trying to straighten our own corner of the world and tugging gently at humankind, urging it to do likewise.

There are definite strains of talent, sensitivity, and creativity that appear repeatedly through the generations: art, music and writing, and directing and acting in films.

And there follows an impressive description of contributions of family members in these areas. Then Jan continues her letter:

> So far we have spoken only on the positive side of sensitivity, but that is not the whole story.
>
> Just as sensitivity makes us perceptive of others, it also makes us vulnerable to them. This has produced personalities in our family who were to varying degrees unable to cope with the rough and tumble world.

Jan goes on to describe the Rice family—now four generations removed: "Our great-great-granddad married two of the three sisters in that family. The whole Rice family was odd, but this second wife was definitely 'over the edge.'" And there follow stories to validate the "over the edge" label! Then Jan's letter goes on:

> For generations after that time, when a family member did something illogical or downright wacky, folks would exchange glances and remark that the person was "just a little Ricey."
>
> A cousin of Grandpa's must have received a more tragic sort of "Riceyness." Although he created a shell of vivacious normality, behind it doubts and despair precipitated suicide at an early age.
>
> That Ricey quality continues to pop up from time to time. Our Mom is an example. Neurotic and difficult as a child, she exhibited bright humor and spontaneity that made her a delightful companion for our Dad for many years. She coped pretty well during the years when she was raising us. But I can remember even then finding her huddled on the attic stairs in the middle of the night trying to hide from the world. In later life she became a recluse, often refusing to see even close members

of the family.

In our generation, I'm reclusive part of the time, but mostly just peculiar. I enjoy people tremendously. They are a necessary spice in my life. But like many spices, too much can precipitate an ulcer. I've learned to hide myself away enough of the time to keep my equilibrium.

I think the Rice strain has been diluted enough in our family by now so that even when it appears it is no longer debilitating. But just to be sure that we all remember that part of our heritage, I dropped one grain of rice into the bright scraps that form the patterns in each one of these kaleidoscopes. That is the fifteenth piece.

Jan went on to share the story of her mother's life—both when her mother was at her best and when she was at her worst:

She hated the concept of right and wrong in social behavior. Many times I can remember her saying that people's actions were not right and wrong, but only different. This broadmindedness gave us the freedom to develop our own interests and to go our own way with confidence.

During her final thirty years her suffering was a shadow over the hearts of all who had known and loved her.

It has taken many years since her death for the memory of what she had become in her final years to fade. That time has come on this her one-hundredth birthday, and I can now remember her once more as the vibrant, spunky, whimsical, fun-loving philosophical spirit I knew.

Her talent in art and writing, and most of all her talent for human understanding, made her remarkable. But as so often happens, talent was coupled in her case with mental instability, so that the sharp-edged sword of sensitivity became aimed at her own heart and destroyed her.

Here is a family coming together after years of silence about certain parts of their family history. They gathered, ready to name and claim the good and the bad:

Ω Hearing stories—perhaps for the first time,

Ω Sharing memories,

Ω Naming the pain and the hurts,

Ω Celebrating the joy and the gifts,

Ω Giving and receiving valued objects that symbolize who they are and who they can become.

This family made a commitment to create connections between the generations. They laughed and cried. They sang (music is a big part of their gift). They remembered. They shared their visions for what the future might be.

It is possible to find ways to link past, present, and future as we explore what it means to celebrate death and life in our families. Story-telling, symbol-claiming, ritual-sharing celebrations can help us claim the past and move into the future empowered because we know more clearly who we are; we know the legacies that are ours to celebrate and to claim, to understand and to choose to change.

Finding Good News through Compassion and Righteousness

For me, the key is *authenticity*. Jenny's service spoke so powerfully because it reflected her own faith and was grounded in the living faith of her family and her church. The "same" service for one who was not grounded in this way would lack integrity and could not do for those grieving what this celebration did. The ritual objects Jan created (her kaleidoscopes) provided a powerful focus for this family's celebration. It had meaning for this family because it was truth-telling and authentic.

Those of us for whom church or synagogue provide a *home* must resist using liturgies and hymns and creating services that presuppose that our stories and traditions offer a home for all in our culture. We do not do anyone a favor by using our faith community's liturgies for people who do not share in that community's life together.

If we continue to be called on in times of crisis and transition by those who claim life in a secular culture, then our task is to work with them to create rituals that truly reflect what they believe and how they live. Our task is to *listen* and then to *be with* people in their times of need. We must avoid offering rituals that may be devoid of meaning for them. We may be able to help them create a ritual that speaks both to them and for them in their time of need.

Let me offer an example. A number of years ago a couple who was living together (at a time when this was less common and less accepted than it is today) asked my husband, Dwight, a pastor and their college religion professor, if he would celebrate their marriage. They wanted him to know, however, that they "don't believe in God!" "Why," he asked, "don't you go to a justice of the peace?" Well, they said, "we do believe marriage is sacred."

Dwight decided that if they were willing to come for three counseling sessions, he would work with them to see if together they could develop a service that reflected who they were and what they believed; and at the same time be a service that he, as a Christian pastor, could perform with integrity. They came; they talked. They wrote a liturgy that had integrity for them. Since their families were

Christian, they agreed that those present could pray for God's blessing on this marriage, even though the couple would not be asked to pray. It was our first experience with an outdoor marriage celebration followed by a picnic of ham sandwiches with horseradish and chocolate wedding cake.

Ten years later, Dwight got a call. "Do you still have a copy of our wedding vows? We want to use them in a covenant renewal service at our church for our tenth anniversary!"

In this case, the planning and celebrating of a marriage covenant that had integrity for this couple—who claimed to be, at least, agnostic—may have been one of the experiences that eventually drew them back into a faith community.

Even if they never had returned to a community of faith, the service was valuable as an expression of care that shared the couple's joy; it also witnessed to a faith community's commitment to truth and to the graciousness of God who loves all people. By not asking them to use rituals and to engage in acts that, for them, would have been a sham, both their integrity and the church's was honored.

Rituals and liturgies that have life and that empower the participants must grow out of the stories and experiences of the people for whom and with whom they are being created. They need to reflect the beliefs and values of the individuals for whom and to whom they speak. Christians who choose to work with folks who do not share their tradition may be able to do so with integrity if they focus together on compassion and righteousness—qualities in which a Christian's faith is grounded.

I once heard Reuel Howe say that a "responsible no" is much better than an "irresponsible yes." To help people engage in acts and speak words that say who they are and where they are in that moment, and to speak of hope within their own personal context, is the greatest gift we can offer.

We invite them to journey in truth and toward Truth with the promise that we believe the God-who-is-truth will be with them. We may be able to bless them through the sacramental acts of *accepting them, listening to them,* and *sharing their pain.* Then they may invite us to help them find ways to name and ritualize an important turning point or loss in their lives. In the spirit of Jesus, Christians are invited to this task.

CHAPTER 5

And The Journey Goes On

Ω

Claiming Our Past and Living into the Future

It is crucial to recognize that deep losses and bittersweet joys stay with us throughout our lives. We need to be sensitive to those "emotionally charged times" that may sneak up on people unawares—the wedding of a friend's child, a baby shower that reminds them of the child their child was never blessed to have, and so many things that trigger a cherished memory or a painful regret.

There are some situations where the need for a ritual act may not, at first, be apparent. For example, think about a couple who discovers at birth that their child is not "the child of their dreams," but is seriously deformed or handicapped. As one ministers with them and encourages them to name their pain and disappointment, their anger and frustration, it may be helpful to invite them to create a liturgy to be shared with an intimate group of family and friends. There is no need for them to feel guilty as they mourn the "death of their hopes and dreams for this child." A ritual may provide a way of freeing them to love and cherish the gift that this special child can become.

Sometimes, we may cause pain by something we say or do. It is important not to withdraw from a relationship because we fear we will do something to cause pain; rather we need to be present with people and let them help us become more sensitive and aware of what their journey is teaching them.

Celebrating death and life in faith communities is what the

journey of faith is all about. As people of faith, we baptize; we bury; we celebrate with those who pass through illnesses and experience health once again; we walk with those whose illnesses lead to and not through "the valley of death." When others are preparing for death and for going to the life we believe is there for them beyond this life, we offer our presence, and we do what we can to help them embrace the pain. We also do our own grief work so that together we might be and become that realm of God on earth, knowing that God cries with us and embraces us with love.

Celebrating death and life in faith communities means that God's Truth must be our truth as well. Services of death and resurrection must not mask reality or hurt those who remain by proclaiming that which they know is not the truth. At the same time, funerals are not the place (nor is there a place!) to lambaste the dead or to try to instill fear in those who remain!

The *United Methodist Book of Worship* offers guidance when a child has died, when there is a stillborn child, or when the community is called to remember people who have experienced untimely or tragic deaths. *Truth* and *compassion* must be intertwined when we work with families who experience death in especially difficult circumstances.

Deep sensitivity to the hopes and dreams, as well as to the fears, anger, and guilt, that people experience in the face of deep loss is crucial. Finding ways to name what is, and to provide safe and hospitable space so that people are free to express their deepest feelings, are gifts that those who claim the gracious love of God are called to offer.

Too often faith communities have failed to invite and honor honesty, and as a result people have experienced judgment and guilt or shame rather than acceptance. Too often those of us in the church are quick to provide "answers" when what people need is someone to listen and to walk into the questions with them.

We must listen to the stories, the feelings, the fears and joys, the dreams unfulfilled and the dreams realized. We must invite family members and close friends to help in shaping the liturgies that are needed to help families and their communities of faith deal with losses and new beginnings. Often, this "work of the people" (for that is what *liturgia* means) can be the beginning of grief work that must be done by those who walk with loved ones through the valley of the shadow of death.

Funerals—services celebrating death and resurrection—may not be the only ritual that is needed, as we have seen. As mentioned previously, students in a class taught by David Otto created a liturgy designed to help a widow or widower feel the support of the faith community as they begin to live more fully after the death of their spouse (Appendix C). Rituals mourning the "death" of one's marriage, one's dream child, or the premature loss of one's ability to conceive and bear a child may be life-giving. It is desirable to find ways to celebrate, ritually, our endings and beginnings as we journey in faith toward God's realm where we will all be made whole.

Commencement

Now we have come full circle. We have shared deeply personal stories of individuals who are seeking to live integrated lives—lives where naming the pain is seen as a part of the healing process. We have reflected on what it means to live sacramentally and how we might create rituals and liturgies that serve as endings and beginnings for us at significant points in our life journeys.

This ending can be a beginning for those who have journeyed with us through these pages. Name your joys and your pains. Claim and tell and retell your stories. Find connections with your stories and the stories of your faith community. Create liturgies or rituals that can help you, and those who share life's faith journey with you, to focus on who and Whose you are and what it means to be

experiencing losses or new beginnings. *Know that our God will be with us!* Our God, the God
>   of Abraham and Sarah and Hagar;
>   of Moses and Miriam;
>   of David and his wives, sons, and daughters;
>   of all of the women and men and children who followed Jesus
>   during his time on earth—listening to his teachings and
>   experiencing how he made the blind to see and the hopeless to
>   have hope;
>   of Jim and Mary, Jennifer and Christopher;
>   of the St. Luke's United Methodist congregation in Dubuque,
>   Iowa;
>   of Robyn and Lorinda;
>   of David and his students;
>   and of you and me—
this God *is faithful.*

This God, whose names are beyond number, will receive our prayers, will walk with us through the valleys, will hold us up when we cannot go on, and will celebrate with us when we dare to walk into the hard questions, seeking, even more than answers, that peace which only God can give. May you be blessed, as I am being blessed, by our compassionate God who cares for all people and the whole creation. So may it be.

APPENDIXES

The people who designed the following liturgies sought to create services for congregations or for small, more intimate groups; they sought to create services that spoke *to them* and *for them* in their particular life situations. They are included here as examples of what you, your family, or your community of faith might be able to create to speak to you and for you.

You may draw on these services as they fit your needs, but their primary purpose here is to stimulate your own creativity. A variety of resources are available from denominations and from individuals, some of which are listed in the bibliography; I encourage you to use them in ways that speak with authenticity and compassion to the situations you need and want to address in worship.

APPENDIX A

St. Luke's United Methodist Church
12th and Main Streets, Dubuque, Iowa
Iowa's Earliest Congregation, 1833
January 14, 1991
10:30 A.M.

A Service of Death and Resurrection
in Memory of

Jennifer Lynn Purdy

Gathering
    Music from the Tower Chime

Prelude:	"Jesu, Joy of Man's Desiring"	J. S. Bach
	"Joy to the World"	Innes
Processional:	"Wind Beneath My Wings"	

        (Theme song from the movie *Beaches* sung by Bette Midler)
The Word of Grace
Greeting
The Word of Promise
      —The Paschal Candle is lit to symbolize the light of Christ
      in the midst of darkness.
      —Water is sprinkled toward the coffin and the gathered
      community as a reminder that our human life is set within

the divine life of Christ that was "put on" at Baptism.
Prayer of Petition for God's Help
*Hymn: "Lord of the Dance"   # 261
             (Stanza 4 is sung slowly and softly in minor.)
*Confession and Pardon
             The Lord be with you.
             And also with you.
Let us pray. (in unison)
             Holy God, before you our hearts are open, and from you no
             secrets are hidden. We bring to you now our shame and
             sorrow for our sins. We have forgotten that our life is from
             you and unto you. We have neither sought nor done your will.
             We have not been truthful in our hearts, in our speech, in our
             lives. We have not loved as we ought to love. Help us and
             heal us, raising us from our sins into a better life, that we may
             end our days in peace, trusting in your kindness unto the end;
             through Jesus Christ our Lord, who lives and reigns with you
             in the unity of the Holy Spirit, one God, now and forever.
             Amen.

             Who is in a position to condemn? Only Christ, Christ who
             died for us, who rose for us, who reigns at God's right hand
             and prays for us. Thanks be to God who gives us the victory
             through our Lord Jesus Christ. Amen.
*Gloria Patri
Prayer for Illumination
First Lesson: Isaiah 40:1–6, 8–11   (Pew Bible, p. 633)
Psalm 23
Second Lesson: Isaiah 40:28–31   (Pew Bible, p. 634)
Special Music: "On Eagle's Wings"   Joncas
             (The people are invited to sing the refrain.
                          It is found at #143.)
New Testament Lesson: 1 Corinthians 12:31*b*-14:1*a*
             (The text is read in Spanish. You may follow along in English
             in the pew Bible at p. 165.)
Special Music: "The Gift of Love"   Hopson
             (This paraphrase of 1 Corinthians 13:1-3 is set to a traditional
             English melody.)

Sermon   Pastor Rex E. Piercy
Naming   Diaconal Minister Ruth Ann Scott
Witness   — Ms. Barbara Ressler, Teacher, Wahlert High School
        — Father John Haugen, Spiritual Director,Wahlert High School
            — Mr. Bernie O'Connor, Counselor, Wahlert High School
    (As Jenny's life is gathered up by the presentation of symbols
    representative of her life, faith, and joy, we hear the music of
                            Pachelbel's Canon.)

The Prayers
    A Prayer Remembering Jennifer   Larry Loeppke
    Commendation
    Thanksgiving
    The Lord's Prayer

Hymn: "Pass It On"   # 895
                (St. Luke's Mountain T.O.P. theme hymn)
*Dismissal with Blessing
*"Hallelujah Chorus" from *The Messiah*   G. F. Handel
*Silence for Prayer
*Music from the Tower Chime "Amazing Grace"
            (The congregation is seated after the Chime as
                the family recesses from the church.)
Recessional: "Oh, But on the Third Day"   W. Marsalis
Postlude: "Sheep May Safely Graze"   J. S. Bach

*The people stand

The family of Jennifer Purdy invites you to join them for a luncheon
in the dining room of the E. Marshall Thomas Fellowship Hall.

Graveside committal service will be conducted at 3:00 P.M. today in
Linn Grove Cemetery near Mt. Vernon.

All the music included in today's service was chosen because of its
special meaning to Jennifer, her family, or her faith community at St.
Luke's.

Assisting today:

Ministers . . . . Every Member of St. Luke's
Pastor . . . . Rex E. Piercy
Diaconal Minister . . . . Ruth Ann Scott
Organist . . . . Ruth Jones
Pianist . . . . Helen Johnston
Chimer . . . . Kathy Reid
Secretary . . . . Eleanor Jach
Vocalists . . . . Andrea Beacham and Larry Loeppke
Acolytes . . . . Leah Piercy and Emily Young
Readers . . . . Dwight W. Vogel and Christopher Purdy
Usher Captain . . . . Robert Lungwitz

APPENDIX B

A Memorial Service
for
Survivors of Abuse upon the Death of the Perpetrator

This is a service of Christian worship for survivors of physical or sexual abuse upon the death of the perpetrator of abuse, when the abuser has also been a family member or close family friend. It is designed to be shared by a small gathering of trusted friends, with or without clergy participation. It could be shared between wife and husband or brother and sister in a very private manner in the home.

This liturgy makes three important assumptions: 1) that the deceased was the perpetrator of abuse and one with whom the survivor(s) had a close, often familial relationship (as in cases of child abuse, spouse abuse, and incest); 2) that the survivor is a Christian; and 3) that the survivor has taken the first steps toward healing the pain of the past and is on the road from being "victim" to becoming "victor" in Jesus Christ.

GREETING
While others have gathered to honor the life and memory of *name,* we confess that this time has brought to us a myriad of emotions that are perplexing. How do we mourn the loss of that which we never really had? How do we mourn the loss of one whom we knew as [specify relationship], but could not trust? How do we mourn the loss of one we loved and hated at once, because our love was manipulated, used, and abused? How do we mourn the death of one with whom we may not have related in years? How do we mourn the loss of one we in reality lost long ago? How do we sing the Lord's song in this strange and fearful land where broken hearts and broken bodies haunt our memory?

PRAYER (in unison)
Lord God, we stand in your presence, knowing that you see our hearts and our lives with greater clarity than we even see ourselves. Accept our anger. Accept our sorrow. Accept our love. Accept our desire for revenge. Accept our desire to forgive, although we find

forgiveness impossible. **Accept our confusion. Accept all that we are
and all that we are becoming in your infinite grace and mercy. Do
not turn your back on us now, for we are only beginning to
understand our great need of your love.**

WORD OF GRACE
God's Word of grace to us is: "Before you were *[father's name]* or
[mother's name], you are Mine—a child of My own creating, precious
in My sight. My grace is sufficient unto the need."

Thanks be to God!

SERVICE OF BAPTISM RENEWAL (optional)
The United Methodist Book of Worship, p.111.
(The vows and sign act of baptism renewal affirm the survivor's
commitment to resist sin and evil in this present day, including the
suffering he/she experienced at the hand of another. The service can
become a commitment to healing, a claim on the conquering power of
grace as manifest in Jesus Christ, and an affirmation that we are indeed
God's own dear child.)

HYMN (see list that follows)

SCRIPTURE LESSON(S) (see list that follows)

WITNESS TO THE WORD (optional)
A meditation on the scriptures may be offered at this time.

SHARING OF OUR JOYS AND PAIN
(Many victims of physical or sexual abuse have memories of good times
as well as memories of the abuse. It is important at the time of death to
tell both and experience the validation of both. This sharing might best
be done by using a formula such as completing the sentence:)

I remember when…. This is a happy/painful memory for me.

Example:
I remember when the whole family went camping at the Grand Canyon.

This is a happy memory for me.

or

I remember when dad took me on fishing trips. This is a painful memory for me.

(Sharing may be in depth or superficial, depending on the comfort level of those who are sharing.)

HYMN

AFFIRMATION OF FAITH
(#881, #883, #884, #885, #887 from *The United Methodist Hymnal* recommended)

RESPONSE: Lord, I believe. Help my unbelief.

COMMENDATION
Almighty God, into your hands we commend the soul of *name,* in sure and certain trust in your justice and your grace, infinite in wisdom and beyond our understanding, through Jesus Christ our Lord. **AMEN.**

PRAYER OF THANKSGIVING
(*The United Methodist Hymnal,* p.875)
God of love, we thank you for all the ways you have blessed us even to this day: For the gift of joy in days of health and strength, and for the gifts of your abiding presence and promise in days of pain and grief. We praise you for home and friends, and for our baptism and place in your church with all who have faithfully lived and died. Above all else we thank you for Jesus, who knew our griefs, who died our death and rose for our sake, and who lives and prays for us. And as he taught us, so now we pray:

THE LORD'S PRAYER

HYMN (optional)

DISMISSAL WITH BLESSING

Suggested Scripture Lessons Appropriate for This Service:
Psalm 63: Longing for God.
Psalm 119:137-144: God's justice brings joy and comfort.
Isaiah 40:27-31: Those who trust in the Lord will find their strength renewed.
Jeremiah 31:29-34: The new covenant and the promise of justice to each according to his sin.
Matthew 25:31-46: The final judgment.
Matthew 28: Jesus' Resurrection.
Romans 8:35-39: Nothing can separate us from the love of God.
Ephesians 3:14-21: The power of Christ's love is given to us.
Hebrews 12:2: The joy of the cross.
Revelation 21:1-4: No more crying, no more pain.

Suggested Hymns Appropriate for This Service:*
O God, Our Help in Ages Past .... #117
God's steadfast care.

On Eagle's Wings .... #143
God's providential care (best when used with verses).

Heal Me, Hands of Jesus .... #262
O Christ, the Healer .... #265
Heal Us, Emmanuel, Hear Our Prayer .... #266
God's healing power.

He Touched Me .... #367
Freedom from the past (be sensitive to the title—for some people this hymn may be inappropriate).

There Is a Balm in Gilead .... #375
This Is a Day of New Beginnings .... #383
Healing for the past; hope for today and tomorrow.

Something Beautiful .... #394
Affirmation/Praise for what God is doing in us.

O God Who Shaped Creation . . . . #443
    Affirmation that we are God's own children and that God is just
    and mourns humanity's evil ways. God is likened to Mother-
    Love (for situations where the father was the perpetrator of
    violence).

Precious Lord, Take My Hand . . . . #474
                    Prayer for God's presence

O Love that Wilt Not Let Me Go . . . . #480
                Affirmation of God's love and grace.

Through It All . . . . #507
            Witness to strength when trusting in God.

I Want Jesus to Walk with Me . . . . #521
                    Prayer for God's presence.

What a Friend We Have in Jesus . . . . #526
            Affirmation of Jesus' presence and care.

When Love Is Found . . . . #643
    Affirmation of those loved ones supporting the bereaved today.
Validation of the pain of betrayed trust and the hope of restoration in
            God's own will and time, which is eternal.

Hymn of Promise . . . . #707

*All hymn numbers are taken from *The United Methodist Hymnal.*

This liturgy is used by permission of Robyn J. Plocher.

APPENDIX C

Ritual of Acceptance of Member
Whose Significant Other Has Died

GATHERING
(The participants should gather around a basin of water. Candles, representing the life and light of Christ in the world, may be lit. Hymns and songs may be sung or played during the gathering.)

OPENING
Leader: With the passing of our loved one, *name,* our community has experienced the departure of a significant member of Christ's holy church. Faith tells us, however, that through the death and resurrection of Christ, this beloved saint has joined the eternity of heaven, purified through the love of Jesus the Christ.

We have celebrated the life of our saint, *brother/sister name.* But now we come together to recognize the grief and pain of this saint's significant other, *name.*

As a community of faith, we come to embrace *name* as our *sister/brother* in Christ. As a family of believers, we come to support *name* in the struggle for understanding, patience, and healing. We come together to ward off loneliness and undue despair. We come to renew our claim to this person as *sister/brother.*

THE RITUAL
(All participants shall approach the basin of water. A member of the group shall read Mark 1:9-11 or Matthew 3:13-17, or both.)

Leader (to the significant other):
In baptism, our beloved saint, *[name of departed],* put on Christ, so in Christ *he/she* was clothed in glory. Likewise, in baptism, *sister/brother,* you put on Christ, so in Christ you stand clothed in glory.

All participants:
In baptism, we have put on Christ, so in Christ we are clothed in

glory. Praise God, the Creator, Redeemer, and Sustainer, who has robed us in the Holy Spirit and named us "children of God."

Leader (to significant other):
Sister/brother, pray with me.
Eternal God, when nothing existed but chaos, you swept across the dark waters and brought forth light. In the days of Noah you saved those on the ark through water. After the flood you set in the clouds a rainbow. When you saw your people as slaves in Egypt, you led them to freedom through the sea. Their children you brought through the Jordan to the land which you promised.

All participants:
Sing to the Lord, all the earth. Tell of God's mercy, each and every day.

Leader:
In the fullness of time you sent Jesus, nurtured in the water of a womb. He was baptized by John and anointed by your spirit. He called his disciples, both men and women, to share in the baptism of his death and resurrection and to make disciples of all nations.

All participants:
Declare the works of God to all nations, the Creator's glory among all people.

Leader:
Great God of all water and earth, pour out your Holy Spirit, and by this gift of water call to *[significant other's name]* remembrance of the grace declared in *her/his* baptism and the family of God to which *she/he* forever will belong.

All participants:
We, too, will remember our baptism. We call you *sister/brother*. We embrace you. We love you. We stand with you forever.

(Leader will ask significant other to kneel. All persons shall gather around *her/him*. In unison, all participants shall dip their fingers in the water. Take fingers and place on cheek of significant other.)

Leader: In your tears, remember your baptism.

All participants:
In your tears, we remember our baptism.

(Dip fingers again. Place fingers on forehead of significant other.)

Leader: In your worry, remember your baptism.

All participants:
In your worry, we remember our baptism.

(Dip fingers again. Surround hands of significant other with your own hands.)

Leader: In this touch, remember your baptism.

All participants:
In this touch, we remember our baptism.

Leader: Let us pray. God, we give thanks for our *brother/sister, name,* whom we remember as a significant member of the family of God. As members of the Body of Christ, all of us promise to support, care, and love our *sister/brother, name,* all the days of *her/his* life and beyond. Amen.

(At this point, the significant other may say whatever *she/he* would like to share with the congregation.)

CLOSING
The God of all grace, who has called us to eternal glory in Christ, establish and strengthen you by the power of the Holy Spirit, that you may live in grace and peace. **Amen.**

From Older Adult Ministry class, David Otto, professor, Centenary College, Shreveport, Louisiana. Used with permission.

APPENDIX D

An Ecumenical Service of Christian Baptism
for Infants and Children in Danger of Death

INTRODUCTION TO THE SERVICE
Hear these words of our Lord and Savior Jesus Christ:
All authority in heaven and on earth has been given to me. Go
therefore and make disciples of all nations, baptizing them in the name
of the Father, and of the Son, and of the Holy Spirit, and teaching
them to obey everything that I have commanded you. And remember, I
am with you always, to the end of the age.
[BOCW, 403, alt./Matthew 28:18-20]

Hear also these words from the Holy Scriptures:
The promise is for you, for your children, and for all who are far
away, everyone whom the Lord our God calls.
[BOCW, 404, alt./Acts 2:39]

In baptism, God claims us and seals us to show that we belong to God.
God frees us from sin and death, uniting us with Jesus Christ in his
death and resurrection. By water and the Holy Spirit, we are born
again and made members of the body of Christ.
[BOCW, 404, alt.]

RENUNCIATION OF SIN AND PROFESSION OF FAITH
Do you reject all that is evil, repent of your sin, and accept the
freedom and power God gives you to resist evil, injustice, and
oppression in whatever forms they present themselves?
I DO.

Do you confess Jesus Christ as your Savior, put your whole trust in his
grace, and promise to serve him as your Lord?
I DO.
[UMBOW, 100, alt.]

Do you believe in God, the Father, Son, and Holy Spirit, who creates, redeems, and sustains all life?
   I DO.

Do you pledge to make God's love known to *name,* by your actions and your words as long as *they* shall live?
   I DO.

THANKSGIVING OVER THE WATER
Pour out your Holy Spirit, to bless this gift of water and *those* who *receive* it, to wash away *their* sin and clothe *them* in righteousness throughout *their* lives, that, dying and being raised with Christ, *they* may share in his final victory. AMEN.

[UMBOW, 101 alt.]

BAPTISM WITH LAYING ON OF HANDS AND ANOINTING
Name, I baptize you in the name of the Father, and of the Son, and of the Holy Spirit. AMEN.

(Laying hands on the child.) The Holy Spirit work within you, that you may live in keeping with God's love for you, both in this world and the next.

(Marking a cross on the child's forehead with oil.)
Name, child of God, you are sealed by the Holy Spirit in baptism and marked as Christ's own forever. AMEN.

[UMBOW, 91]

LORD'S PRAYER
Let us join together in prayer, that our *sister/brother* may hear the prayer that Jesus taught all his disciples to pray:
   Our Father, who art in heaven. . . .

BENEDICTION
The God of all grace, who has called us to eternal glory in Christ, establish you and strengthen you by the power of the Holy Spirit, that you may live in grace and peace. AMEN.

[UMBOW, 102]

SOURCES

BOCW Presbyterian Church (U.S.A.). *Book of Common Worship Prepared by the Theology and Worship Ministry Unit for the Presbyterian Church (U.S.A.) and the Cumberland Presbyterian Church.* Louisville: Westminster/John Knox Press, 1993.

UMBOW *The United Methodist Book of Worship.* Nashville: United Methodist Publishing House, 1992.

Lorinda H. M. Hoover, O.S.L., designed this service while doing a unit of CPE (Clinical Pastoral Education) at Northwestern Memorial Hospital in Chicago, Illinois, during the summer of 1994. It is designed as a modular service. Various sections may be omitted, as circumstances and the pastoral intuition of the officiant dictate. It is shared with her permission.

A SELECTED BIBLIOGRAPHY

This bibliography of selected resources is intended for those who seek ways both to mourn and to celebrate death, as they keep on keeping on.

Dying and Death
The books in this section invite people to explore the dying process and to consider ways we might assume more responsibility for the way we live and die.

Harwell, Amy. *Ready to Live: Prepared to Die*. Wheaton, Ill.: Howard Shaw Publishers, 1995.

Hill, T. Patrick, and David Shirley. *A Good Death: Taking More Control at the End of Your Life*. Reading, Mass.: Addison-Wesley Publishing, 1992.

Kübler-Ross, Elisabeth. *On Death and Dying*. New York: Macmillan, 1970.

———. *Death: The Final Stage of Growth*. New York: Simon & Schuster, 1986.

Nuland, Sherwin B. *How We Die: Reflections on Life's Final Chapter*. New York: Alfred A. Knopf, 1994.

Quill, Timothy E. *Death and Dignity: Making Choices and Taking Charge*. New York: W. W. Norton, 1993.

Being with and Caring for the Dying and Bereaved
These books may be helpful to people who desire to be with and to offer support both to persons who are dying and to their families. Some are especially designed for congregations who are seeking to develop caring ministries with the dying.

Callanan, Maggie, and Patricia Kelley. *Final Gifts: Understanding the Special Awareness, Needs, and Communications of the Dying*. New York: Poseidon Press, 1992.

Dobihal, Fr. Edward F., and Charles William Stewart. *When a Friend Is Dying: A Guide to Caring for the Terminally Ill and Bereaved*. Nashville: Abingdon Press, 1984.

Donnelly, Katherine. *Recovering from the Loss of a Child*. New York: Berkeley Publishing Group, 1994.

Edelman, Hope. *Motherless Daughters: The Legacy of Loss*. Reading, Mass.: Addison-Wesley Publishing, 1994.

Edelstein, Linda. *Maternal Bereavement*. New York: Praeger Publishers, 1984.

Krementz, Jill. *How It Feels when a Parent Dies*. New York: Alfred A. Knopf, 1988.

Kübler-Ross, Elisabeth. *On Children and Death*. New York: Macmillan, 1985.

Menten, Ted. *Gentle Closings: How to Say Goodbye to Someone You Love*.

Philadelphia: Running Press, 1992.

Meyer, Charles. *Surviving Death: A Practical Guide to Caring for the Dying and the Bereaved.* Mystic, Conn.: Twenty-Third Publications, 1991.

Nouwen, Henri J. M. *Our Greatest Gift: A Meditation on Dying and Caring.* San Francisco: HarperSanFrancisco, 1994.

Sanders, Catherine M. *How to Survive the Loss of a Child.* Rocklin, Calif.: Prima Publishing, 1992.

————. *Surviving Grief...and Learning to Live Again.* New York: John Wiley & Sons, 1992.

Staudacher, Carol. *Beyond Grief: A Guide for Recovering from the Death of a Loved One.* Marietta, Ga: Active Parenting Publishers, 1987.

————. *Men and Grief: A Guide for Men Surviving the Death of a Loved One.* Oakland, Calif.: New Harbinger Publications, 1991.

Webb, Nancy, ed., *Helping Bereaved Children: A Handbook for Practitioners.* New York: Guilford Press, 1993.

Books about or for Children and Youth

This section includes books to be read by and/or with children, which are marked with an asterisk (*), and books written for adults. Some of these books are old and are probably available only from libraries. They are listed here in the hope that they will be useful to some. Those I have marked with a double asterisk (**) are books that I highly recommend for families and church libraries.

*Barker, Peggy. *What Happened when Grandma Died.* St. Louis, Mo.: Concordia Publishing House, 1984.

**Coerr, Eleanor. *Sadako and the Thousand Paper Cranes.* New York: Putnam, 1977.

Cohn, Janice. *I Had a Friend Named Peter: Talking to Children about the Death of a Friend.* New York: William Morrow, 1987.

*De Paola, Tomie. *Nana Upstairs and Nana Downstairs.* New York: Puffin Books, 1978.

Fitzgerald, Helen. *The Grieving Child: A Parent's Guide.* New York: Simon & Schuster, 1992.

Furman, Erna. *A Child's Parent Dies.* New Haven and London: Yale University Press, 1974.

*Gootman, Marilyn E. *When a Friend Dies: A Book for Teens about Grieving and Healing.* Minneapolis: Free Spirit Publishing, 1994.

**Grollman, Earl A. *Talking about Death: A Dialogue between Parent and Child.* Boston: Beacon Press, 1976.

Grollman, Sharon Itya. *Shira: A Legacy of Courage.* Garden City, N.Y.: Doubleday, 1988.

*Harbaugh, Hollie J., and Roger F. Miller. *When My Grandma Died.* St. Louis:

CBP Press, 1986.

**Lichtman, Wendy. *Blew and the Death of the Mag.* Monroe, Utah: Freestone Publishing, 1975.

Lonetto, Richard. *Children's Concepts of Death.* New York: Springer Publishing, 1980.

*Mellonie, Bryan, and Robert Ingpen. *Lifetimes: The Beautiful Way to Explain Death to Children.* New York: Bantam Books, 1983.

*Murray, Gloria, and Gerald G. Jampolsky, eds. *Another Look at the Rainbow.* Berkeley, Calif.: Celestial Arts, 1995.

*Nobisso, Josephine. *Grandma's Scrapbook.* Old Tappan, NJ: Simon & Schuster Children's, 1991.

*———. *Grandpa Loved.* Old Tappan, NJ: Simon & Schuster Children's, 1989.

*Paterson, Katherine. *Bridge to Terabithia.* New York: HarperCollins Children's Books, 1987.

*Rofes, Eric E., ed. *The Kids' Book about Death and Dying: By and for Kids.* New York: Little, Brown, 1985.

*Sanford, Doris. *It Must Hurt a Lot: A Child's Book about Death.* Sisters, OR.: Questar, 1985.

Schaefer, Dan and Christine Lyons. *How Do We Tell the Children? Helping Children Understand and Cope with Separation and Loss.* New York: Newmarket Press, 1993.

*Simon, Norma. *The Saddest Time.* Morton Grove, Ill.: Albert Whitman, 1986.

*Stickney, Doris. *Water Bugs and Dragonflies: Explaining Death to Children.* Cleveland: Pilgrim, 1982.

*Thomas, Jane. *Saying Good-bye to Grandma.* Boston: Houghton Mifflin, 1990.

*Vigna, Judith. *Saying Goodbye to Daddy.* Morton Grove, Ill.: Albert Whitman, 1991.

*Viorst, Judith. *The Tenth Good Thing about Barney.* New York: Aladdin Books, 1987.

Vogel, Linda Jane. *Helping a Child Understand Death.* Ann Arbor: Books on Demand, 1975.

Waas, Hannelore, and Charles A. Corr. *Helping Children Cope With Death.* Bristol, PA: Hemisphere Publishing, 1984.

Death of Infants and Children
The pain of losing a baby or a young child is great. These resources may be helpful at some point to those who are dealing with their grief from such a loss.

Cole, Diane, "It might have been: Mourning the unborn." *Psychology Today,* July 1987.

Donnelly, Katherine Fair. *Recovering from the Loss of a Child.* New York: Berkeley Publishing Group, 1984.

Hickman, Martha Whitmore. *I Will Not Leave You Desolate: Some Thoughts for Grieving Parents.* Nashville: Abingdon Press, 1994.

Johnson, Sherry E. *After a Child Dies: Counseling Bereaved Families.* New York: Springer Publishing, 1987.

Klass, Dennis. *Parental Grief: Solace and Resolution.* New York: Springer Publishing, 1988.

Panuthos, Claudia, and Catherine Romeo. *Ended Beginnings: Healing Childbearing Losses.* Westport, CT: Greenwood Publishing Group, 1984.

Rando, Therese A., ed. *Parental Loss of a Child.* Champaign, Ill.: Research Press, 1986.

Schwiebert, Pat. *Still to be Born.* Portland, Ore.: Perinatal Loss, 1993.

AIDS and Dying

HIV and AIDS are issues that many people hope they will never have to encounter. These issues, however, have touched and will touch many of us and many in our communities of faith. These books are informative and myth-destroying, and they offer words of compassion and hope for all who seek to reach out to people who live with the reality of HIV and AIDS.

Alyson, Sasha, ed. *You Can Do Something about AIDS.* Boston: Stop AIDS Project, 1988, 1990.

Ascher, Barbara Lazear. *Landscape without Gravity: A Memoir of Grief.* New York: Delphinium Books, 1993.

Brown, Joe, ed. *A Promise to Remember: The Names Project Book of Letters.* New York: Avon Books, 1992.

Brown, Marie and Gail M. Powell-Cope. *Caring for a Loved One with AIDS: The Experiences of Families, Lovers, and Friends.* Seattle, WA: University of Washington Press, 1992.

Crowther, Colin E. *AIDS: A Christian Handbook.* Valley Forge, PA: Trinity Press International, 1991.

Dietz, Steven D., and M. Jane Parker Hicks, M.D. *Take These Broken Wings and Learn to Fly: The Support Book for Patients, Family, and Friends Living with AIDS.* 2nd ed. Tucson: Harbinger House, 1992.

Donnelly, Katherine. *Recovering from the Loss of a Loved One to AIDS: Help for Surviving Family, Friends, and Lovers Who Grieve.* New York: Fawcett Book Group, 1995.

Hay, Louise L. *The AIDS Book: Creating a Positive Approach.* Carlsbad, Calif.: Hay House, 1988.

Quakenbush, Marcia, and Sylvia Villarreal, M.D. *Does AIDS Hurt? Educating Young Children About AIDS.* Santa Cruz, Calif.: ETR Associates, 1992.

Reed, Paul. *Serenity: Support and Guidance for People with HIV, Their Families, Friends, and Caregivers.* 2nd ed. Berkeley, Calif.: Celestial Arts,

1995.
Shelp, Earl E., and Ronald H. Sunderland. *AIDS and the Church: The Second
    Decade.* Louisville, KY: Westminster John Knox Press, 1992.
Sunderland, Ronald H., and Earl E. Shelp. *Handle with Care: A Handbook for
    Care Teams Serving People with AIDS.* Nashville: Abingdon Press, 1990.
Wiener, Lori S., Aprille Best, and Philip A. Pizzo, comps. *Be A Friend: Children
    Who Live with HIV Speak.* With a foreword by Robert Coles. Morton Grove,
    Ill.: Albert Whitman, 1994.

Death through Suicide
Why? These resources may provide a starting point for those who must deal with
the suicide of a loved one or friend.
Robinson, Rita. *Survivors of Suicide.* North Hollywood, CA: Newcastle
    Publishing, 1992.
Stillion, Judith M., Eugene E. McDowell, and Jacque H. May, eds. *Suicide
    across the Life Span: Premature Exits.* Bristol, PA: Hemisphere Publishing,
    1996.
Wrobleski, Adina. *Suicide: Survivors. A Guide for Those Left Behind.*
    Minneapolis: Afterwords, 1994.
———. *Suicide: Why? 85 Questions and Answers about Suicide.* Minneapolis:
    Afterwords, 1995.

Exploring the Theology of Suffering and Death
These books offer a beginning point for those who desire to explore ways people
of faith have sought to make meaning in the face of suffering, death, and grief.
Hauerwas, Stanley. *Naming the Silences: God, Medicine, and the Problem of
    Suffering.* Grand Rapids, Mich.: William B. Eerdmans Publishing Co., 1994.
Hessert, Paul. *In Lieu of Meaning.* New York: Crossroads/Continuum, 1991.
Kushner, Harold S. *When Bad Things Happen to Good People.* Avenal, NJ:
    Random House Value, 1990.
Rahner, Karl. *On the Theology of Death.* New York: Herder and Herder, 1961.
Weatherhead, Leslie. *The Will of God.* Nashville: Abingdon, 1987.

Planning Services for Remembering and Celebrating Life and Death
The following resources provide prayers, hymns, and liturgies, as well as a
variety of ways of ordering services of worship. People may use them to design
services that speak both *to others* and *for others* at those times in their lives
when they experience deep loss and are struggling to find hope. Individuals are
encouraged to find ways to authentically express the myriad of emotions that
engulf people when they are brought face to face with dying and death.

The Book of Common Prayer. According to the Use of the Episcopal Church. New York: Seabury Press, 1979.

Book of Common Worship Prepared by the Theology and Worship Ministry Unit for the Presbyterian Church (U.S.A.) and the Cumberland Presbyterian Church. Louisville: Westminster/John Knox Press, 1993.

Book of Worship: United Church of Christ. Cleveland: United Church of Christ Office for Church Life and Leadership, 1986.

Duck, Ruth. *Finding Words for Worship: A Guide for Leaders.* Louisville: Westminster John Knox, 1995.

Duck, Ruth, and Maren C. Tirabassi, eds. *Touch Holiness: Resources for Worship.* Cleveland: Pilgrim Press, 1990, 156–163.

Fink, Peter E., S.J. *Alternative Futures for Worship: Anointing of the Sick.* Vol. 7. Collegeville, Minn.: Liturgical Press, 1987.

Lutheran Book of Worship: Ministers Desk Edition. Minneapolis: Augsburg Fortress Publishing House, 1978.

Moffat, Mary Jane. *In the Midst of Winter: Selections from the Literature of Mourning.* New York: Random House, 1992.

Sloyan, Virginia, ed. *A Sourcebook about Christian Death.* Chicago: Liturgy Training Publications, 1990.

Sublette, Kathleen, and Martin Flagg. *Final Celebrations: A Guide for Personal and Family Funeral Planning.* Ventura, Calif.: Pathfinder Publishing of California, 1992.

The United Methodist Book of Worship. Nashville: Abingdon, 1992.

The United Methodist Hymnal. Nashville: The United Methodist Publishing House, 1989.

Williamson, Marianne. *Illuminata: Thoughts, Prayers, Rites of Passage.* New York: Random House, 1994.

Autobiography and Biography—Grief and Loss

Sometimes the most helpful thing we can do is read an autobiographical account—to walk into someone else's life story and find those places where their story touches ours. These books have the power to touch us in life-giving ways.

Broyard, Anatole. *Intoxicated by My Illness and Other Writings on Life and Death.* New York: Crown Publishing Group, 1992.

Coughlin, Ruth. *Grieving: A Love Story.* New York: HarperCollins, 1994.

L'Engle, Madeleine. *The Summer of the Great-Grandmother.* San Francisco: HarperSanFrancisco, 1980.

Lewis, C. S. *A Grief Observed.* San Francisco: HarperSanFrancisco, 1994.

Martin, John D. *I Can't Stop Crying: It's so Hard when Someone You Love Dies.* Buffalo: Firefly Books, 1992.

Nouwen, Henri J. M. *In Memoriam.* Notre Dame, In.: Ave Maria Press, 1980.

————. *Letter of Consolation.* San Francisco: HarperSanFrancisco, 1990.

Rose, Xenia. *Widow's Journey: A Return to the Loving Self.* New York: Henry Holt, 1995.

Rutledge, Carol Brunner. *Dying and Living on the Kansas Prairie: A Diary.* Lawrence, Kans.: University of Kansas Press, 1994.

Williams, Terry Tempest. *Refuge: Unnatural History.* New York: Random House, 1992.

Reference Books
These books provide additional bibliographic information for those who are seeking additional resources.

Benson, Hazel B. *The Dying Child: An Annotated Bibliography.* Westport, CT: Greenwood Publishing Group, 1988.

Pyles, Marian S. *Death and Dying in Children's and Young People's Literature: A Survey and Bibliography.* Jefferson, N.C.: McFarland, 1988.

Waas, Hannelore, and Charles A. Coor, eds. *Helping Children Cope with Death: Guidelines and Resources.* Bristol, PA: Hemisphere Publishing, 1984.

ACKNOWLEDGMENTS

Excerpts from *Book of Common Worship*. Copyright © 1993 Westminster/John Knox Press. Used by permission of John Knox Press.

Excerpt from "Lord of the Dance" by Sydney Carter. Copyright © 1963 by Stainer & Bell, Ltd. Used by permission of Hope Publishing Company, Carol Stream, IL 60188. All rights reserved. Used by permission.

Material from "Heritage Day." Used by permission of Jan Conn.

"An Ecumenical Service of Christian Baptism for Infants and Children in Danger of Death" Used by permission of Lorinda Hoover.

"Prayer." Used by permission of Larry Loeppke.

"Ritual of Acceptance of Member Whose Significant Other Has Died." Used by permission of David Otto.

Excerpts from "Homily." Used by permission of Rex Piercy.

"Liturgy for a Memorial Service for Survivors of Abuse upon the Death of the Perpetuator." Used by permission of Robyn J. Plocher.

From "Witness to Jenny." Used by permission of Barbara Ressler.

"Our Jenny." Used by permission of Helen Schaub.

Excerpts from "An Act of Naming." Used by permission of Ruth Ann Scott.

Material in Chapter 2 and "For Christ's Sake, (Don't) Get Out 'a the Cemetery." Used by permission of James Stewart.

Excerpts from "A Service of Death and Resurrection" from *The United Methodist Book of Worship*. Copyright © 1992 The United Methodist Publishing House.